Proceedings of the Institution of Mechanical Engineers

Conference

Engineering for Profit from Waste

15 March 1988
Crest Hotel
Coventry

Sponsored by
Power Industries Division of the Institution of Mechanical Engineers

Co-sponsored by
County Surveyors Society
Institution of Chemical Engineers
Institution of Civil Engineers
Institute of Energy

IMechE Conference 1988–1

Published for the Institution of Mechanical Engineers
by Mechanical Engineering Publications Limited

First published 1988

The illustration on the front cover is a diagram of the Landfill Gas Abstraction and Piping Scheme — Bidston Marsh. It is reproduced by courtesy of the Department of Energy Efficiency and by Coal Processing Consultants (Project File number 216).

Contents

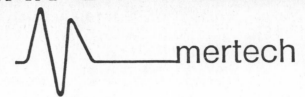
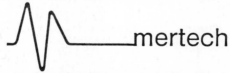

The Institution of Mechanical Engineers

The primary purpose of the 76,000-member Institution of Mechanical Engineers, formed in 1847, has always been and remains the promotion of standards of excellence in British mechanical engineering and a high level of professional development, competence and conduct among aspiring and practising members. Membership of IMechE is highly regarded by employers, both within the UK and overseas, who recognise that its carefully monitored academic training and responsibility standards are second to none. Indeed they offer incontrovertible evidence of a sound formation and continuing development in career progression.

In pursuit of its aim of attracting suitably qualified youngsters into the profession — in adequate numbers to meet the country's future needs — and of assisting established Chartered Mechanical Engineers to update their knowledge of technological developments — in areas such as CADCAM, robotics and FMS, for example — the IMechE offers a comprehensive range of services and activities. Among these, to name but a few, are symposia, courses, conferences, lectures, competitions, surveys, publications, awards and prizes. A Library containing 150,000 books and periodicals and an Information Service which uses a computer terminal linked to databases in Europe and the USA are among the facilities provided by the Institution.

If you wish to know more about the membership requirements or about the Institution's activities listed above — or have a friend or relative who might be interested — telephone or write to IMechE in the first instance and ask for a copy of our colour 'at a glance' leaflet. This provides fuller details and the contact points — both at the London HQ and IMechE's Bury St Edmunds office — for various aspects of the organisation's operation. Specifically it contains a tear-off slip through which more information on any of the membership grades (Student, Graduate, Associate Member, Member and Fellow) may be obtained.

Corporate members of the Institution are able to use the coveted letters 'CEng, MIMechE' or 'CEng, FIMechE' after their name, designations instantly recognised by, and highly acceptable to, employers in the field of engineering. There is no way other than by membership through which they can be obtained!

C02/88

The role of mathematical models in evaluating the provision of waste treatment facilities

M P PUGH, BSc(Eng), CEng, MICE, MIWEM, PEng
Binnie and Partners, Redhill, Surrey

SYNOPSIS The identification of the most cost-effective long term solution to waste management within a county or regional area is exceedingly complex. The paper describes how the use of mathematical models can focus the waste disposal authority's view on the current and future operation of disposal facilities, enabling proper comparisons of costs and opportunities to be made among the diverse range of waste treatment technologies being promoted today.

Specific reference is made to HARBINGER, the Harwell waste management model, which is gaining acceptance among waste disposal authorities as a versatile tool for use in the preparation of waste disposal plans. The paper describes the flexibility of this model to cope with a wide range of waste management options and its ability to respect operational constraints set by the user.

Within these constraints the model calculates least cost solutions for any given waste disposal strategy against a range of objectives for cost minimisation, and reports facility usage, traffic movements and distribution of costs among a number of waste management agencies. The model simulates the opening up, operation and closing down of any selected waste treatment or disposal facility and can report the net present value of a plan over periods of up to 20 years by discounted cash flow techniques.

1.   INTRODUCTION

Waste management is a major industry with an annual turnover in the United Kingdom probably exceeding £1 billion. The majority of these costs are borne by the public sector which in 1986 amounted to £393M for waste collection and £218M for waste disposal (Ref 1). Under the Control of Pollution Act (COPA) 1974 the responsibility for controlled waste disposal in England is vested in the County Councils while in Scotland and Wales the responsibility for this function is at the district authority level.

County Councils in England are responsible under COPA for preparing and maintaining statutory Waste Disposal plans covering the disposal of household, commercial and industrial wastes expected to arise over a minimum period of ten years. The task of preparing such a plan is extremely onerous. The 'average' non-metropolitan English county may be categorised as having the following key characteristics:

Population	747 000
Area (km^2)	3 120
District authorities	8
County owned Landfill sites	8
Waste treatment facilities	
(including transfer stations)	2
Civic Amenity Sites	10

The majority of the currently operating landfill sites will have been exhausted within such a ten year planning period and replacement sites, both known, and as yet unidentified, will be brought into use. In addition, financial and environmental pressures on these disposal authorities will result in replacement or additional waste treatment facilities being built and operated, primarily to serve the districts, which are responsible for collection of household waste.

The basic problem facing any waste disposal authority attempting to prepare a Waste Disposal Plan may be summarised as:

"Given an expected pattern of waste production, the costs of building and operating various treatment and disposal facilities and the costs of transporting wastes to those facilities: how does the authority select the facilities which should be built together with their location, capacity and time for implementation."

It is implicit in the search for this preferred plan, that the 'Best Practicable Environmental Option' must also be optimal in terms of total cost. However, assessment of future costs is very complex.

The larger sites and more sophisticated waste treatment facilities are often very expensive to develop and there is a need to demonstrate a balance of savings in waste collection and transportation costs against large or frequent capital expenditures for disposal facilities, and possibly enhanced facility operating costs. The problem is compounded by a number of uncertainties in the factors which affect the economics and viability of any strategy, for example changes in population and waste quantities or composition; changes in transportation routes; susceptibility of future capital costs to currency fluctuations; and sensitivity of future operating costs to, for instance, labour or fuel costs.

Clearly the task of evaluating fully a range of possible alternative strategies would require an enormous amount of staff effort for the average county waste disposal authority and there would be a temptation to restrict the range of options considered and only to evaluate fully the first plan found to meet the operational constraints set.

Such a strategic planning problem, however is amenable to solution by computer based mathematical modelling, enabling a wide range of disposal options to be investigated fully and on a consistent basis. However it should be remembered that no model can take account of every real world aspect of a system, and compromises must be made between reality and ease of calculation. The system must be capable of being specified by explicit mathematical relationships. Any simplification necessary to achieve this must either have an insignificant effect on the results (output) from the model, or its effect should be known to, and compensation made by the user of the model.

2. MATHEMATICAL MODELS

A wide range of mathematical models have been developed for waste management planning since the late 1960's, varying in complexity and degree of sophistication. A comprehensive literature review of the use of models in the planning of solid waste management was carried out by D. C. Wilson in 1977 and updated in 1981 (Ref 2). Early models were generally restricted to optimising the location(s) of a single type of facility, for a single time period, with no constraint on operating capacity, whereas the more recent models may be used to choose a set of facilities from a limited number of selected locations.

The level of sophistication of these models is reflected in the way in which capital and operating costs are treated, and how the effect of time is modelled. Waste management models also vary in their scope and flexibility, e.g.:

-   in the scale of the problem that they can handle (the number of waste arising sources and sinks);

-   in the range of treatment facilities that can be modelled;

-   in the ability to apply operating constraints on facilities; and

-   in the ability to carry out sensitivity analyses.

Probably the most sophisticated waste management model currently in use is that developed for the Hong Kong Government by Binnie & Partners (Hong Kong) in association with the Harwell Laboratory. Developed in 1982/83 and in constant use since, the Hong Kong model has facilitated an exhaustive comparison of options

for the disposal of waste, taking account of likely real increase in certain costs and has included all the complex issue involved in allocation of wastes to existing facilities and future planned replacements (Ref 3). The Hong Kong model has since been developed further by the Harwell Laboratory and has been copyrighted under the name HARBINGER (Ref 4).

3. THE HARBINGER MODEL

3.1 Structure of the model

One of the main features of this model which makes it significantly more advanced than earlier models is that it is fully interactive, having been specifically designed for use by waste disposal staff themselves, whose task it is to build up and evaluate alternative waste disposal plans. In order to facilitate this, this model has been developed as an integrated suite of eight programs, or sub-models, which may be used sequentially to build up and assess a waste disposal strategy. These are used, in turn:

-   to calculate the quantities of waste requiring treatment or disposal;

-   to select the list of facilities to be made available;

-   to derive the shortest travel times through the road system and the unit costs of hauling waste;

-   to estimate the unit costs of treating and/or landfilling waste at each of the selected facilities; and

-   to determine the utilisation of each facility within the operating constraints set by the user which is the most economic overall, taking account of all transport, treatment and disposal costs.

In total over 30 "reports" are available to the waste manager, which can be viewed at the VDU screen or printed for later reference. These provide detailed information on the issues in waste management covered by each sub-model.

The scope and sophistication of mathematical models may be judged by reference to Table 1 which sets out some of the key dimensions of the database used in the installation of the model at Walsall for the West Midlands Waste Disposal Co-ordinating Authority.

Further background to the structure of this model may be found in Reference 5.

3.2 Data requirements

HARBINGER requires a considerable amount of data in order to model fully the movement of wastes through the system over a period of 10 to 20 years. However the data required are reasonably accessible to a waste disposal authority, and it may be argued that they are no more than would be required to prepare a fully evaluated waste disposal plan by hand.

Table 1 indicates only the principal areas of data required to define the waste management

TABLE 1 Typical data dimensions of HARBINGER
(as installed at Walsall MBC)

WA WASTE ARISINGS SUB-MODEL	
Waste arisings areas (excluding districts)	220
Districts (for coarser modelling)	15
Regions (for summary reporting)	1
Basic primary waste types (eg Household, commercial, industrial)	3
Components for each basic type (eg inert, putrescible)	2
Time periods considered (for modelling up to the planning horizon	5
SS STRATEGY SELECTION SUB-MODEL	
Secondary waste types (process residuals)	15
Existing treatment plants	30
Existing landfill sites	15
Potential landfills	20
Potential technologies	10
Potential sites (which combined with a technology defines a potential waste treatment plant)	25
Feasible operating capacities at any facility	4
Unit Costs (for global calculations)	5
Unit revenues (from recovered products, including energy)	12
Depots (for overnight parking of vehicles)	15
TN TRANSPORT NETWORK SUB-MODEL	
Road network nodes	800
Additional nodes (sources, sinks, depots)	340
Barge transfer origin nodes	15
Rail transfer origin nodes	5
Alternative road networks	2
TC TRANSPORT COST SUB-MODEL	
Collection Practices	7
FC FACILITY COST SUB-MODEL	
Cost data for each existing and potential treatment or disposal facility may be entered in up to five user-defined formats. Limits on maximum numbers of cost components (columns) and cost centres (rows) per format are:	
Initial (capital) cost components (major + minor)	8
Initial (capital) cost centres (major + minor)	12
Annual cost components (major + minor)	16
Annual cost centres (major + minor)	5
Terminal (closing down) cost components	5
Terminal (closing down) cost centres	5
Occasional costs (for major plant refurbishment or further site development work) can be specified by year of occurrence from first use of facility for any feasible operating capacity.	
Maximum lifetime of a facility (in years)	50
AO ALLOCATION OPTIMISATION SUB-MODEL	
Responsible agencies (for cost allocation)	20

system. It is recognised that data relating to private sector activities are unlikely to be a comprehensive or as available as those for the public sector. Nevertheless the generation, transportation, treatment and disposal of private sector wastes and the use of the private sector for management of publicly collected wastes may be modelled to the extent that data may be obtained.

By way of example, the following discussion on some of the data requirements for the Facility Cost sub-model will indicate the level of sophistication to which the model can be used.

In order to be able to take account of the effect of economy of scale, data are required for each potential waste treatment or disposal

facility corresponding to at least three design or 'feasible' daily operating capacities.

The data files prepared by the user contain four types of cost data, plus expected revenues. The four sets of costs are:

Initial costs   -   representing the capital cost to design and construct the facility;

Annual costs   -   the recurrent costs of operation and maintenance;

Occasional costs – reflecting
major capital related costs
such as substantial
refurbishments required
during the lifetime of the
facility; and

Terminal costs – representing
any capital costs associated
with the closing of the
facility

The level of detail with which, say, the initial cost of a facility is specified may be chosen by the user. In general, costs may be specified in matrix format, with each row representing an identifiable part of the facility (or cost centre) and each column a particular type of cost (or cost component).

Cost data for each item in a matrix can be supplied in the form of lump sums; as factors on other costs; or in the case of annual costs, as the number of units of a particular resource, such as number of men or kWh of electricity, plus the unit cost of this resource (the latter being specified in a general unit cost file input to the Strategy Selection sub-model). Figure 1 is a typical output report from the model giving key economic data for a particular strategy, escalated to the year 1988.

Figure 2 illustrates the level of detail for initial costs for a large incinerator which might be derived from preliminary design studies, while Figure 3 illustrates a similar level of detail for annual costs for such a facility. Where such detail is not available the cost matrices may be reduced in size to, if necessary, one-by-one dimensions, i.e. lump sums for each of the stated 'feasible capacities'.

Physical data are also required for each facility, defining, inter alia:

- those types of waste which
  may be delivered to the facilities;

- any constraint on quantities or proportion
  of each acceptable waste type;

- products recovered from the waste stream;

- the process residuals; and

- the design lifetime.

4. THE USE OF HARBINGER TO EVALUATE WASTE TREATMENT PROCESSES

One of the most difficult exercises to carry out by hand is the determination of how best a potential waste treatment facility may be introduced into an established waste disposal system. The size, type and location of any new facility, and the timing of its introduction in the system will each have a fundamental effect on the operation and cost of the waste disposal plan. In developing alternative strategies for consideration, the waste disposal authority should consider a wide range of options for any such facility.

The selection exercise may be carried out to at least two levels of detail in order to weed out progressively those candidate technologies which prove not to be of financial or operational advantages to the system.

In the first instance, expressions of interest might be invited from a wide range of waste treatment technology promoters, covering the more straightforward waste transfer station to the state-of-the-art resource recovery facilities. Using budget estimate lump sums for the Initial, Annual, Occasional and Terminal costs and key operating data supplied by the respondents, a wide range of alternative technologies may be modelled.

For each option HARBINGER would be used to consider the introduction of the new facility into the system, the pattern of usage of that facility throughout the planning period and the total net present value, determined by DCF calculation, of the plan using that facility. Figure 4 is an extract of a summary report showing the average usage of a set of waste treatment and disposal facilities considered over the first five years of a 20 year planning period. It shows for instance that facility 505 – a new transfer station – operates most economically (for the entire system) within the constraints set by the user. Had the usage been forced to meet the minimum requirement (as for facility 31 where the model has respected the constraint to route at least 600 TPD through the plant), it would indicate that a cheaper overall system would result from the lesser use of that facility.

However, the determination of the optimum use and cost of a particular facility, and of the overall system cost for a strategy based on the use of a particular set of facilities, goes only part of the way towards the evaluation of a candidate technology. There are may other aspects of waste management which can (and should) be considered using HARBINGER. These aspects, which are potential advantages frequently cited by proponents of waste treatment facilities, include:

(1) The impact on the waste collection authority

The central location of a waste handling facility can make substantial long term savings to the collection authority in reduced vehicle fleet and crew requirements, lower operating costs due to shorter hauls and even reduced incidence of tyre punctures through not using a landfill site. The model can indicate all of these potential savings.

(2) The reduction in traffic movements

Centrally located waste treatment facilities permit bulk haulage of waste to disposal sites. Where waste reduction is achieved by incineration or resource recovery, even fewer loads of process residuals need be transported to landfill. The model will determine for any type of facility, for any length of working day, the bulk haulage fleet requirements for delivery of process residuals to any chosen disposal site.

4

(3) The savings in landfill space

Often a waste disposal authority is forced to consider seriously the provision of a waste treatment facility due to an acute shortage of locally available landfill capacity. The model can be used to demonstrate the valuable extension of a landfill's lifetime.

(4) Flexibility in disposal route

Bulk haulage by road of process residuals gives the waste disposal authority considerable choice in the use of landfill sites which may not otherwise be possible due to excessive haul distances for the refuse collection vehicles. The model can indicate the most cost effective choice of disposal site for process residuals, or alternatively will indicate the costs for using any specified disposal site.

Certain disbenefits may also be modelled, either explicitly or implicitly, for example, externalised costs associated with heavy vehicle movements, such as rural road deterioration, noise and nuisance to residents can be taken into account by adding an appropriate 'cost' per vehicle movement on the affected parts of the road network. Similarly, other social costs, reduction of property values and the sterilisation of land by virtue of hazardous waste deposition can be taken into account as a 'cost component' in preparing the 'initial cost' data (Figure 2) for any particular site.

By modelling a range of alternative strategies through a reasonably long planning period (up to 20 years or more) the long term implications of capital intensive waste reduction systems on, say, the availability of landfill sites and on the savings in cost of waste transportation can be explored.

Sensitivity analysis

Having determined how the candidate technologies compare with each other in the context of the whole system based on the budget cost and physical data supplied by the proponents of the various systems, it would be prudent to carry out an analysis of the sensitivity of the total system cost and the robustness of the plan to various items of data. These analyses, which can be carried out quickly and easily using mathematical models would investigate the effect of correcting over-optimistic assessments of :-

- the capital and operating costs of the proposed facilities;

- the quantity of residuals produced or the payload and operating costs of the bulk haulage vehicles used to transport these residuals;

- the security of the market for recovered resources; and

- in the event of a total collapse in the market resulting in the financial failure of the facility, how the system would cope with the sudden unavailability of the facility.

Based on this broad assessment of options,

the waste disposal authority will be in a better position to judge the characteristics of the waste treatment facility most suited to its needs. A formal Requests for Proposals may then be issued to selected firms.

Data from these proposal could then be used in further modelling to identify which proposal would be most beneficial to the waste disposal plan. At this level, sensitivity analyses might be expanded to determine, for instance the effect of significant changes in the cost of labour or the cost of energy against the general rate of inflation.

5. HARDWARE REQUIREMENTS

Computer programs are limited to some extent in their scope by the computers on which they are intended to be mounted. The large, sophistication models such as HARBINGER require considerable data storage capacity and high computation speed. For this reason the larger mainframe installations are generally required to run these models; for example HARBINGER is currently running on IBM and ICL mainframes.

With the rapid evolution of powerful micro-computers, many waste management models could be tailored to run on such industry standards as IBM PC XTs and ATs, provided the 'size' of the problem being modelled can be limited. For instance, there is a version of HARBINGER for use on the above micro-computers in conjunction with the Lotus 1-2-3 spreadsheet package. Such developments aim to bring the capability of mathematical modelling of waste disposal systems within the financial reach of the smaller authorities responsible for waste management planning.

6. CONCLUSIONS

Many waste disposal authorities are having to take decisions to make substantial capital investment in waste treatment facilities in order to provide a satisfactory basis for medium to long term disposal of wastes. The range of options available for waste treatment together with the complexity of the waste management systems in operation within the most English counties severely inhibits the full evaluation of alternative waste disposal strategies by hand.

Computer based mathematical models can be used to assess the suitability of a wide range of alternative waste treatment facility both quickly and consistently, and to a level of thoroughness which would be practically impossible by hand.

REFERENCES

(1) Chartered Institute of Public Finances and Accountancy Waste Collection Statistics 1985-86 Actuals, P4 and Waste Disposal Statistics 1986-87 Estimates, P7

(2) D.C. Wilson. Waste Management - Planning, Evaluation, Technologies Oxford University Press, 1981 p45-62

(3) R.W.M. Hoare, J.E. 'Boxall & D.T.W. Wong, Role of a strategic planning model in waste management in Hong Kong. Proceedings of the First Asian Pacific Conference on Pollution

in the Metropolitan Environment. Elsevier
Press 1985.

(4) HARBINGER is a trade mark of the UKAEA

(5) Rushbrook P.E and Pugh M.P Waste management
planning - an illustrated description of
HARBINGER, the Harwell Waste Management
Model Wastes Management, June 1987

```
--------------------------------------------------------------------------------
SS: ECONOMIC DATA - CURRENT UNIT COSTS AND PRODUCT REVENUES.          (COSTS)
EXISTING LANDFILLS & TREATMENT PLANTS + NEW TRANSFER STA(505)
--------------------------------------------------------------------------------

            UNIT COSTS AT YEAR 1988
            ------------------------
                UNIT NAME                  CURRENT COST   % GROWTH/ANNUM
    1   LABOUR COST PER YR                   9623.68         2.000
    2   LABOUR COST-MANDAY                     38.49         2.000
    3   ELECTRICITY   £-KWH                     0.06         3.000
    4   DIESEL FUEL   £-L                       0.32         3.000
    5   FUEL OIL      £-L                       0.27         3.000
    6   SUPR. COST PER YR                   11704.48         2.000
    7   SUPR. COST-MANDAY                      46.82         2.000

            UNIT REVENUES AT YEAR 1988
            --------------------------
            PRODUCT        UNIT NAME       CURRENT VALUE   % GROWTH/ANNUM
    1   INCINERATOR ASH      TE                 0.51         1.000
    2   COMPOST              TE                 2.55         1.000
    3   FERROUS METAL        TE                10.20         1.000
    4   BURNT FE METAL       TE                 5.10         1.000
    5   STEAM                GJ                 3.18         3.000
    6   ELECTRICITY          KWH                0.04         3.000
    7   METHANE              GJ                 3.18         3.000

            OTHER ECONOMIC DATA
            -------------------
    WORKING DAYS PER ANNUM      260.0
    DISCOUNT RATE ( % )         4.000
    OVERTIME COST FACTOR        1.3
    BASE YEAR                   1986
```

Fig 1   Current values of unit costs and revenues

All costs in £ million

| Cost Component | Civil Engineering | | | Preliminary | Design | | |
Cost Centre	E&M (1)	General (2)	Foundations (3)	Site Investigation (4)	& General (5)	& Supervision (6)	Contingency (7)
10 Site works, utilities	0	.75	0				
20 Waste reception	1.07	.51	.60				
30 Waste processing		4.09	.68	0.004 of (2 + 3)	0.15 of (1 + 2 + 3)	0.08 of (1 + 2 + 3)	0.15 of (1 + 2 + 3 + 4 + 5 + 6)
31 fixed plant	13.11						
32 mobile plant	0.5						
40 Gas cleaning and stack	9.55	.77	.20				
50 Energy recovery	17.74	.19	0				
60 Residuals handling	2.68	1.00	.30				
70 Miscellaneous equipment	8.20	0	0				
Sub totals	52.40	7.31	1.78	.04	9.22	4.92	11.35
TOTAL							87.02

Sub totals and total calculated by model and carried forward to DCF calculation.

Data may be entered, alternatively, in simpler form eg as lump sum (£87 m) or a 1 x 2 matrix such as E+M
and Civil Works costs.

Fig 2   Initial cost matrix suggested for use in Harbinger for a large incinerator

	Cost component	Basis of estimate	Comment
10.	Operating and maintenance	No. of men	Includes all grades up to works supervisors. All shifts
20.	Local supervision	0.4 of (10) or no. of men	Includes all grades from Asst Inspector upwards. Figure of 40% based on costs converted to factor.
30.	Overtime and allowances	0.1 of (10 + 20)	Cost converted to factor.
40.	Local administration	0.05 of (10 + 20)	Includes all clerical and supplies staff, and generally one Workman, plus office supplies. 5% based on cost converted to (%) factor.
50.	Departmental supervision	0.032 of (10 + 20)	Cost calculated as per accounts, converted to factor.
60.	Electricity	kWh/tonne	Estimated directly.
70.	Operating supplies	Lump sum per annum	Oil, grease etc estimated directly.
80.	Maintenance parts	Lump sum or % of total capital cost	Estimated directly as % of E & M initial cost.
90.	Departmental administration	0.076 of (10 + 20)	Taken from a factor given in Accounts.
100.	Materials handling overhead	0.03 of (70 + 80)	% of operating supplies, fuel plus general maintenance.
110.	Central administration	0.04 of (10 to 100)	Taken from a factor given in accounts.
120.	Contingency	0.15 of (100 to 110)	Can be reduced for existing facilities.

Fig 3 Suggested format for entering the annual costs in Harbinger

SS: FACILITY USAGE BY WASTE TYPE (TPD) AFTER PERIOD INCREMENT. (REMAINING)
EXISTING FACILITIES & NEW TRANSFER STATION (505)

TREATMENT/TRANSFER FACILITY 32 JAGDEAN INCIN

WASTE TYPE	MAX & MIN LIMITS IN LAST PERIOD		USED	UNUSED	MAX & MIN LIMITS FOR NEXT PERIOD	
10	1000.0	0.0	700.0	300.0	1000.0	0.0
20	200.0	0.0	200.0	0.0	200.0	0.0
ALL	1000.0	900.0	900.0	100.0	1000.0	900.0

TREATMENT/TRANSFER FACILITY 34 BELCHILL COMPOST

WASTE TYPE	MAX & MIN LIMITS IN LAST PERIOD		USED	UNUSED	MAX & MIN LIMITS FOR NEXT PERIOD	
10	365.0	0.0	365.0	0.0	365.0	0.0
ALL	365.0	350.0	365.0	0.0	365.0	350.0

TREATMENT/TRANSFER FACILITY 505 KEEP DYKE TRANSFER-CONT-ROAD

WASTE TYPE	MAX & MIN LIMITS IN LAST PERIOD		USED	UNUSED	MAX & MIN LIMITS FOR NEXT PERIOD	
10	1200.0	350.0	371.3	828.7	1200.0	0.0
20	1200.0	350.0	660.6	539.4	1200.0	0.0
ALL	1200.0	800.0	1031.9	168.1	1200.0	0.0

DISPOSAL FACILITY 44 TEDWORTH BAY

WASTE TYPE	MAX & MIN LIMITS IN LAST PERIOD		USED	UNUSED	MAX & MIN LIMITS FOR NEXT PERIOD		
10	1868.1	0.0	131.5	1736.7	0.0	0.0	EXPIRED
20	1868.1	0.0	65.6	1802.5	0.0	0.0	EXPIRED
30	1868.1	0.0	0.0	1868.1	0.0	0.0	EXPIRED
61	1868.1	0.0	383.6	1484.5	0.0	0.0	EXPIRED
71	1868.1	0.0	255.5	1612.6	0.0	0.0	EXPIRED
81	1868.1	0.0	1031.9	836.2	0.0	0.0	EXPIRED
ALL	1868.1	0.0	1868.1	0.0	0.0	0.0	

DISPOSAL FACILITY 44- LIFETIME HAS NOW EXPIRED

DISPOSAL FACILITY 44 DELETED FROM SELECTION
DEPOT FOR DISTRICT 1010 CHANGED FROM 2 TO 4
DEPOT FOR DISTRICT 1040 CHANGED FROM 2 TO 4
PERIOD INCREMENTED FOR STRATEGY 2 MPP
THE NEW PERIOD IS 2, FOR YEARS 1993 - 1996
N.B. TRANSPORT NETWORK AND OTHER SUB-MODELS MUST BE RERUN
SS READY

PRIMARY WASTE TYPES:-

* 10 HOUSEHOLD-COMMERCIAL	11 CIVIC AMENITY	* 20 INDUSTRIAL
21 HIGH CV INDUSTRIAL	* 30 CONSTRUCTION	31 HIGH CV CONSTRUCTION

SECONDARY WASTE TYPES:-

* 61 INCINERATOR ASH	* 71 PULVERISED REJECTS	72 COMPOST
* 81 CONTAINERS BY ROAD	82 CONTAINERS BY BARG	83 CONTAINERS BY RAIL
84 PULVERISED BY ROAD	91 CRUSHED WASTE	92 OFFLOADED CONTAINERS

* INDICATES A SELECTED WASTE

Fig 4 Extract from full report printed after using 'Increment' command

C03/88

Where there's muck there's gas

B J W MANLEY, BSc, MSc, PhD, CEng, MInstE, **H S TILLOTSON**, BSc, MSc and **D C WILSON**, MA, DPhil, CChem, MRSC
Environmental Resources Limited, London

SYNOPSIS   The economics of landfill gas abstraction require careful and thorough consideration. Exploitation of the gas must always be considered but viability can only be assured when an accurate forecast of gas generation rate can be made.

Reliable forecasts depend upon realistic site simulations and these in turn require input of information which has been measured directly on site.

The effectiveness of the simulation can be improved by reducing the errors in the site assessments and by adopting a new approach to quantifying the performance of the site.

A new variable, specific gas yield, is introduced to meet these criteria.

NOTATION

$A_{b/l}$	Surface area of gas well boundary layer
A_i	Surface area of individual well 'zone'
C_o	Quantity (concentration) of waste
C_{val}	Calorific value
$(C_{val})_i$	Calorific value, individual well
E	Gas collection efficiency
k	Degradation velocity constant
n	Number of gas wells
P	Energy selling price
Q	Gas flowrate
R	Annual revenue
t_{pa}	Annual waste input tonnage
$t_{\frac{1}{2}}$	Waste decay half-life
W	Total quantity of waste
Y	Gas yield
$(Y*)_i$	Individual-well specific gas yield
$(Y*)_o$	Site-well specific gas yield

1.   INTRODUCTION

In recent years there has been a growing recognition that landfill gas generation can be both a potential environmental hazard and a marketable energy resource. Emissions of gas on-site may cause serious disruption to site restoration, while gas migration may result in:

-    property damage due to explosions or fire caused by the build-up of gas in confined spaces such as culverts, trenches and foundations;

-    loss of life due to asphyxiation in culverts, trenches or manholes;

-    crop die-back on or adjacent to landfill sites; and

-    odour problems.

1.1   Environmental Control

The explosive potential of landfill gas has become a major issue with recent incidents such as Loscoe, Derbyshire receiving widespread publicity. This and other risks to the environment have lead to the Royal Commission on Environmental Pollution (11th report HMSO, Dec 1985) and the Hazardous Wastes Inspectorate (1st report January 1985) recommending that landfill site operators should be obliged to provide adequate gas control.

Landfill sites situated in strata allowing the migration of gas (e.g. gravels, sandstones and fissured rocks) pose the greatest threat to the environment. Lateral migration may be prevented by:

-    impermeable barriers such as clay, bentonite, grout or plastic liners;

-    passive venting by means of a perimeter trench filled with coarse aggregate; or

-    gas abstraction by pumping from one or more gas wells. Usually the gas is burned off using a flare system.

If gas abstraction is required, then the cost of the pumping may in some cases be reduced by sale or exploitation of the recovered gas.

1.2   Exploitation Possibilities

The utilisation of landfill gas has been shown to be economically viable in several schemes within the UK. Utilisation may take the form of:

- direct use of gas; or

- conversion to electricity.

Direct combustion schemes include brick-kiln firing (Winlow J.A., (1986)), boiler firing (Brown S.P., (1986)) and cement-kiln firing (McKendry P.J., (1986)). Electricity generation schemes include the internal combustion gas engines at Stewartby (Moss H.D.T., and Manley B.J.W., (1986)).

Whilst utilisation is important to maximise landfilling profits, it is essential that gas emissions are controlled. The basic irony of gas abstraction is that maximising emission control will reduce the quality of the gas, and thereby its saleability. In order to provide a balance, the exploitation scheme must be designed carefully with an understanding of the factors affecting gas production, enabling a realistic production rate to be estimated. This leads to the need for an integrated design incorporating gas wells, the capped surface, the collection pipework, compression plant and energy user, with the implications of their interactions well understood.

1.3   Economics

In order to justify any gas extraction scheme, a market survey is required to assess the saleability of the gas, together with such variables as quantity of waste in place, energy sale price and probable gas recovery efficiency.

The economics of gas abstraction are heavily influenced by maintenance and operating costs and by the relative costs of other energy sources such as oil and natural gas.

The actual threshold for exploitation viability depends on the gas user as well as other variables.

The Energy Technology Support Unit (ETSU) for the Department of Energy have been instrumental in providing an assessment of the total potential landfill gas resource for the UK. Environmental Resources Limited have been commissioned by ETSU to undertake this study.

2.   GAS PRODUCTION RATE FORECASTING

Whenever gas control or exploitation schemes are required, it is essential that the economic isssues are examined as thoroughly as possible. Choice of equipment types and operational details will have great bearing on the net gas abstraction costs. Design must be structured and must be based upon a sound initial estimate of the likely availability of gas.

2.1   Estimation of the Viability of Gas Abstraction

Exploitation of landfill gas must always be considered because the revenue obtained will offset the costs of simple environmental control. Whether or not a site is large enough to warrant a full survey of the local energy market is difficult to assess. In order to do this, an estimate of the order of magnitude of the likely gas production rate is required.

The simplest approach to generate a forecast of this type is to assume a linear production rate law and to use this to examine realistic ranges of the key revenue influencing variables. This equation can be defined as:

Revenue = Gas Volume x Gas-to-energy Conversion Factor x Sale Price of Energy

$$R = Y.E.P.t_{pa} \qquad (1)$$

Expected ranges for these variables are:

$0.05 < P < 0.30$ £/therm (or equivalent)
$20\% < E < 100\%$
$10^3 < t_{pa} < 10^7$ tonnes/year

The expected gas yield, Y, is the subject of great debate and a number of different values have been quoted (ANL (1981), Rees (1980), Stegmann (1986)). For a forecasting exercise, a mid-range figure of 200 m^3 of gas per tonne of waste can be assumed. Errors in this assumption have been offset by purposely choosing a wide range for the collection efficiency term, E. The simplest way to examine equation (1) is to draw a graph, or 'surface plot' and highlight the area of interest. This is shown in Figure 1.

The use of the graph is illustrated by the following example:

- site annual input, say 280,000 tonnes;

- expected energy sale price 0.12 £/therm;

- assumed gas recovery efficiency 40%.

This defines point 'A' in Figure 1, from which the expected annual revenue of approximately £475,000 can be read off.

The foregoing analysis makes no allowance for the rate at which gas is generated - a factor which is vital to realistic forecasting. This sort of data can only be obtained by examining a site in some detail; this will generally require on-site gas pumping trials.

2.2   Site Evaluation Studies - Gas Pumping Trials

The mechanism of refuse degradation is fairly well understood. Pacey (1986) has outlined a number of processes which predominate in anaerobic digestion and Emberton (1986) has examined the biological characteristics which govern this process. However, the kinetics cannot easily be quantified, and as a result, rigorous mathematical modelling is not possible.

The most readily available method of gathering this type of information, which is vital for gas forecasting, is to measure the performance of the site itself.

The usual approach is to install a small gas pumping rig which is fitted with suitable flow and pressure monitoring equipment. The site is then assessed in terms of:

- well head flow versus suction characteristics;

- well radius of influence, or the area from which the gas is abstracted by the gas well. Normally determined by monitoring at large distances from the well; and

- gas composition as a function of elapsed time from the start of pumping.

Information obtained from the trials may be used to calculate a gas production rate.

This general approach suffers from several major deficiencies, related primarily to the radius of influence. These are:

o Defining and measuring a 'radius' assumes that the gas flow distribution around the well is uniform. Very near to the well, essentially this will be true, further away, however, will show large deviations.

o The measurements that are used to determine the radius of influence are obtained from pressure sampling probes, or piezometers. The measurements are inherently unreliable owing to a very small absolute magnitude coupled with a relatively high measurement error.

o Pressures measured at large distances from the gas well will be an indication of the net effect of three separate, but interrelated factors:

  - diffusion of individual gas components within the gas mixture;

  - bulk flow caused by pressure gradients resulting from atmospheric pressure changes; and

  - the negative (and very small) pressure field directed towards the gas well.

o Edge effects, which result in discontinuities in the gas flow field are not allowed for.

o No account is taken of the vertical pressure gradients, i.e. those that act in parallel to the axis or centreline of the gas well. These will be small close to the well, but larger further away.

o Comparison between sites, or even separate sections of an individual site cannot be made.

2.3 Pumping Trials - New Approach to Data Evaluation

In order to improve the information required to generate an accurate gas production forecast, two approaches could be adopted:

- develop a reliable and truly representative laboratory method to enable degradation kinetics to be quantified; and

- modify the approach to the gas pumping trials, particularly the concept of radius of influence.

Because of the complexity of the refuse-to-gas process as well as the preponderance of 'uncontrolled' and random factors associated with the landfill site itself, the former approach is unlikely to lead to improved forecasting.

For the latter approach to succeed, a new variable must be defined which will overcome the deficiencies described in Section 2.2. Initially, the methodology used in conducting the pumping trial would not change; only the analysis would be different. However, if a new variable, once defined and assessed, proved to be both reliable and more accurate, then the pumping trial could be modified and perhaps simplified.

2.4 Specific Gas Yield - A New Variable

The underlying principle of gas pumping trials is to assess the performance of a gas well and correlate this to site behaviour. The key to improving the accuracy is to reduce the relative error in the measurements and to eliminate factors associated with the random nature of the site. This can be achieved most readily by examining the region very near to the gas well in which:

- pressure changes are large and the response time to a change imposed at the well head, i.e. when the well is 'switched-on', for example, is small; and

- the radial distribution of flow will be essentially uniform.

To take into account edge effects such as air ingress through the surface or at the site boundaries, consideration of 'power flux' and not simply volumetric gas flow should be used. Power flux can be calculated easily from total flow and gas sample analyses - i.e. the concentration of CH_4.

This type of variable is a 'well yield' and the concept can be extended by relating it to the amount of waste in place. This should be the total amount and not the amount which is actually 'supplying' gas to the well - which in itself is indefinable. This specific gas yield can be defined as:

Specific Gas Yield $(Y^*)_0 = \dfrac{Q.C_{val}}{A_{b/l}.W}$ (2)

The area term, A has been subscripted 'b/l' (boundary layer) because the flux will approach a uniform radial distribution only in a thin region adjacent to the outside surface of the well casing. However, it is reasonable to assume that uniform radial distribution will persist some distance from the well, say of the order of 1m.

Hence, to compare two different sites, a power flux can be calculated for both at a given (small) distance from the well.

For installations with multiple well arrangements, the complex interactions that occur when several wells are in use simultaneously may be investigated by examining the ratio:

$$\frac{(Y^*)_i}{(Y^*)_0} = \frac{Q_i \, (C_{val})_i / A_i.W}{Q.C_{val}/A_{b/l}.W} \quad (3)$$

Taking $A_i = A_{b/l}$, Equation (3) reduces to:

$$\frac{(Y^*)_i}{(Y^*)_0} = \frac{Q_i \, (C_{val})_i}{Q.C_{val}} \quad (4)$$

where $\quad Q.C_{val} = \displaystyle\sum_{i=1}^{n} Q_i \, (C_{val})_i \quad (5)$

and n = number of wells in use.

In this case, $(Y^*)_i$ represents a specific gas yield for an individual well and $(Y^*)_0$ represents the specific gas yield for the site as a whole.

Values for $(Y^*)_0$ for a number of active gas abstraction schemes are given in Table 1.

Data obtained in this way may be used as a basis for simulations from which a forecast of gas availability may be made.

3.   REFUSE DEGRADATION SIMULATION

In the previous section (see 2.2), the complexity of refuse degradation was outlined. However, if empirical data can be obtained to allow assessment of an overall rate of reaction, then the process can be simulated with reasonable accuracy by a 'first order' process.

3.1   First Order Models

Models based on first order kinetics represent the simplest solution to refuse decay. They are based upon an equation of the form:

$$\frac{dC_0}{dt} = f(e^{-kt}) \quad (6)$$

The actively decaying quantity is given by C_0 and k is a velocity constant defining the overall rate of reaction.

Several approaches to the solution of this first order differential equation can be made:

- From first-hand experience of actual landfill, assume values for decay 'half-lives' where half life is given by

$$t_{\frac{1}{2}} = \frac{1}{k} \ln (2) \quad (7)$$

- From pumping trial data, estimate the gas production rate and by trial and error determine a value of k to fit.

Hoeks (1983) has examined decay processes in this way and suggests that waste can be divided into four fractions:

- readily degradable $(t_{\frac{1}{2}} = $ a year) e.g. food wastes;

- moderately degradable $(t_{\frac{1}{2}} = 5$ years) e.g. garden wastes;

- slowly degradable $(t_{\frac{1}{2}} = 15$ years) e.g. paper, wood; and

- non-degradable.

Integration of equation (6) will give the quantity of gas production to be expected. To model the landfill, a series of integrations must be performed for individual sections of the site - 'unit cells' - and the solutions summed over a staggered time base. The number of cells needs to be large to enable close representation of the whole site. The technique used to sum these cells is basically a column matrix addition.

3.2   Relating Simulation Studies to Practice

So often, computer simulations either bear no relation to practice or are so complex that simple checking and verification of the result is not possible. For landfill simulation, a first order approximation applied to a small cell could be checked with reasonable accuracy by means of gas pumping trials. In addition, the trials can be designed to gather data which could be used to characterise a particular site which will have its own waste-in-place mix, hydrogeology, capping material, etc. Using characteristics, such as refuse porosity, specific gas yield, specific gas production rate, the model may be extended to the other cells which make up the site as a whole.

However, because of the nature of refuse decay i.e. a fairly sensitive micro-biological process governed by a number of factors, the forecasted production rates could deviate from actuality to a large extent - particularly towards the end of gas production.

In general, for schemes exploiting the gas, the large scale production phase occurs early on and for this period, the forecast is likely to be a close approximation.

4. LANDFILL DESIGN

4.1 Site Planning and Design

At the initial site planning and design stage, factors such as the landfilling technique, rate of input, waste mix, temperature and moisture content of the waste and the restoration of the site must be considered to maximise gas production. Additionally, in order to fully exploit the gas, the design of the abstraction system and plant must be considered in conjunction with the site design.

With the growing concern over gas and leachate migration, containment sites either natural or lined are favoured in many areas. Sites in the slow or rapid dispersal categories require some form of migration control, which can be either passive or active.

A good landfilling practice is to rapidly restore small areas of sites, commonly using a cellular bunded method to minimise leachate production, thereby decreasing moisture content and reducing waste temperatures. The use of steel wheeled compactors to achieve good compaction rates also increase gas generation by reducing the potential for aerobic activity. The depth of a site has bearing on the 'rapid restoration' method. The deeper the site the greater the infill rate required to achieve the restoration, resulting in the need for stringent initial planning.

In order to maximise gas production from an early stage, the progressive installation of gas wells (vertical and/or horizontal) or trenches should be planned.

The economics of gas abstraction are heavily influenced by maintenance and operating costs, therefore the need for an accurate assessment of potential gas production is important at the planning stage in order that the correct position and frequency of gas wells and correct equipment may be determined to maximise efficiency. In cellular filling, knowledge of the position of the bund walls is essential in the planning of the extraction system.

The relative merits of horizontal compared with vertical wells is debatable. In conditions where a rising leachate level occurs a horizontal arrangement of pipework may be rendered inoperable. Conversely in sites where installation occurs at the end of the site life, with a high leachate level, horizontal wells achieve a greater effectiveness than vertical.

A further consideration is the effect of settlement. At the planning stage the restoration contours must be designed to allow for settlement in order to achieve the planned final restoration. Settlement also provides problems of integrity for horizontal pipes, even if encased in a coarse aggregate. The use of flexible joints goes some way to alleviate this problem. For vertical wells, connections to the surface pipework should have flexible connections, again to allow for settlement. Good compaction during filling reduces the effect of settlement.

The placing of at least 1 m of clay as a capping surface for completed sites is also important, decreasing the infiltration of rainwater and reducing the intrusion of air. This in turn decreases leachate generation. The doming of the site allows the shedding of rainwater, slopes of 1:20 to 1:30 are typical. A good peripheral drainage system is important in such cases.

As degradation rates and hence gas generation rates, are affected by moisture content and the temperature of the waste, the controlled addition of liquid, whether water or recirculated leachate may be used to enhance gas production.

4.2 Integrated Design Approach

To design a cost effective gas collection system, the sizes of individual components, particularly pipework must be as near optimal as possible. A large proportion of the capital expenditure will be tied up with gas wells and collection pipework, as a result considerable care is required when designing this part of the system

Design of the abstraction network requires information on two fundamentally different gas flow regimes:

- collection network pipe flow;

- below ground flow through the site itself.

Designing a pipe network to connect well defined nodes or gas wells is a relatively straightforward engineering exercise. However, for a landfill gas abstraction scheme there are two factors which make the task more complex:

- for optimum recovery, gas well positions are not easy to specify; and

- movement of the landfill surface caused by settlement means that low spots in the network could occur. These are prone to collect condensate and can result in blocking of large sections of the network as a whole.

For these reasons, an interactive computer-aided solution is required. The logic for such a scheme is suggested in Figure 2. The main logic flow is concered with designing the network. Two possibilities for initiation are indicated:

- a simple approach which assumes gas flows for pre-determined well positions; and

- a more rigorous approach which models firstly the gas production process and which would call upon site-derived data such as specific gas yield and well interaction factors.

The routine also assumes that the landfill surface has been designed separately. This could be done, for example, by surface modelling computer software. The gas network design would have to be linked to this by means of an external programme interface. The result would be a fully integrated and interactive programe that would specify:

- well positions;

- collection network layout;

- pipework sizes; and

- final or capped surface contours, with built-in settlement allowances.

5. ECONOMIC ASPECTS

The length of time over which a landfill site is operational, coupled with the relatively slow waste degradation process mean that careful planning is essential. For the economics to be cost effective, a forecast which is as reliable as possible, must be available. From this, equipment selection and sizing, and an operational strategy can be found. The overall cost of recovering gas from a landfill site may be found by summing a series of components. These will comprise equipment and running costs.

5.1 Typical Equipment Costings

The major components of a typical gas abstraction installation with associated costings are:

Application	Environmental Control (£)	Exploitation (£)
Gas Wells + Well Heads	12,500	12,500
Collection Pipe Networks	17,000	17,000
Water Removal	5,500	5,500
Compression Unit + Drive	3,500	8,500
Secondary Water Removal + Filtration	1,000	13,500
Instrumentation + Control	2,500	2,500
Excess Gas Flaring	9,500	9,500
Metering	-	4,500
Civils	11,500	11,500
TOTAL	**63,000**	**85,000**

These figures are based upon a plant designed to handle up to 750 m^3 hr^{-1} of gas. The environmental control scheme would have a centrifugal blower and only rudimentary water removal, whereas the exploitation scheme would require (say) a Roots-type blower, refrigeration-type water removal and full metering and monitoring.

5.2 Operating Costs

The major component costs for operation of such a plant would be:

Application	Environmental Control (£)	Exploitation (£)
Energy Input Costs	5,040	12,600
Maintenance Costs	3,150	4,250
Capital Depreciation	3,270	7,850
Labour and Attendance Costs	3,750	5,625
TOTAL	**15,210**	**30,325**

Environmental control scheme:- 20kW continuous electrical input, 350 days per year; maintenance at 5% of capital; depreciation assumes 5 year plant life, excluding wells and pipework; Labour costs 1 man-day per week at £75/day.

If a 15 year installation life is assumed, then life-cycle costings for the two options are:

Application	Environmental Control (£)	Exploitation (£)
Life Cycle Costing	291,150	539,875
Cost per m^3 Gas	0.003	0.006
Income (gas sales at 0.12 £/therm)	-	0.021*

* assumes a nearby user replacing a low grade coal.

To determine costings for a real system, the output from the gas forecast must be used to define an initial plant capacity and a planned series of additional units to cater for the extra gas which becomes available with time. The equipment sizings and power inputs will be derived from the computer-aided integrated design routine.

5.3 Developments and Markets

There are a number of options for the exploitation of landfill gas and some of these are receiving Department of Energy funding under the 'Energy Efficiency Demonstration Scheme'. Richards (1986) describes these.

To be cost effective, an exploitation scheme generally requires a relatively near user and preferably a modest sized constant base load. The economics of such schemes need to be very carefully considered, particularly in the light of the current deflated world energy prices.

Novel alternatives, which are likely to receive increasing attention in the future will concentrate on on-site use. Possible applications could include:

o Electricity generation to provide:

- power to run the gas abstraction equipment;

- on-site facilities and amenities;

- to run leachate pumping and handling systems.

o Gas firing producing heat to provide:

- special waste (sewage filter cakes) drying;

- treatment of recycled and recovered materials such as scrap alloy melting;

- destruction of toxic wastes such as pesticides;

- bulk volume reduction of poorly degradable materials before landfilling to prolong the life of the site.

6. CONCLUSIONS

Landfill gas generation from the decomposition of municipal waste can be both a problem and a source of profit. Uncontrolled emissions of gas can seriously disrupt site restoration while gas migration can give rise to nuisance complaints, property damage and even loss of life.

It is vital that gas emissions are controlled, but in so doing expenditure incurred must be minimised. One method of reducing the cost is to utilise or exploit the energy of the gas. Herein lies a conflict: maximising emission control will tend to reduce the quality of the gas, and thereby, its saleability.

To maximise the contribution of gas to landfilling profits, careful attention to design, and above all, a sound gas quantity forecast are necessary. This leads to the concept of 'integrated design' - gas wells the capped surface, collection pipework, compression plant and the energy user - all must be well understood. The underlying foundation of any scheme must be a realistic estimate of the rate of gas generation. This requires a high level computer simulation model based on existing knowledge of refuse degradation, supplemented by empirical information obtained directly from the site under consideration.

To justify gathering data suitable for using in the simulation, an order of magnitude for the revenue availability can be found by examining simple variables such as quantity of waste in place, energy sale price and probable gas recovery efficiency. This is conveniently achieved by plotting a 'nomogram' which can be used to define quickly the potential for energy sales.

The economics of gas abstraction are heavily influenced by maintenance and operation costs and these must be monitored and controlled to maximise profit.

Many types of equipment are available, but for a particular application each component must be specified precisely, and it is only by adoption of an integrated design methodology that the right choice can be made.

Future gas exploitation schemes are likely to be centered more on on-site usage and the landfill will be run in conjunction with the gas control scheme. Possible applications within this concept include the pretreatment of non-degradable wastes before they are landfilled. This will increase the lifetime of the site and thereby improve profitability.

These ideas are reflected in the title of this paper - 'Where there's muck there's gas'.

7. REFERENCES

Angonne Nat. Lab., June 1981. 'State of the Art Methane Gas Enhancement in Landfills'. DOE W-31-109ENG38. (ANL)

Brown, S.P. 'Landfill Gas Abstraction/Use - Operational Schemes at CPC Sites'. Energy from Landfill Gas. Proc. Joint UK/US Department of Energy Conference, Solihull, 23-31 October 1986. pps 281-284.

Emberton, J.R. 'The Biological and Chemical Characterisation of Landfills'. Ibid. pps 150-163. 'Hazardous Waste Management An Overview'. Hazardous Wastes Inspectorate, 1st Report, June 1985.

Hoeks, J. 'Significance of Biogas production in Waste Tips'. Waste Management and Research 1(4) (Dec 1983). pp 323.

McKendry, P. 'Operational Schemes at Blue Circle Industries plc Landfill Sites'. Energy from Landfill Gas. Proc. Joint UK/US Dept. Energy Conference, Solihull, 23-31 Oct. 1986. pps 304-314.

Moss, H.D.T. Manley, B.J.W. 'Review of Landfill Gas Field Projects' Shanks and McEwan (Southern) Limited. Ibid. pps 225-236.

Pacey, J.G. 'Factors Influencing Landfill Gas Production', Ibid. pps 51-59.

Rees, J.F. 'The fate of carbon compounds in the landfill disposal of organic matter'. J. Chem. Tech. Biotechnol 30 (1980) p162.

Richards, K.M.; Rushbrook, P.E. 'Landfill Gas Exploitation - Demonstration Schemes in the UK'. Energy from Landfill Gas. Proc. Joint UK/US Dept. Energy Conf., Solihull, 23-31 October 1986). pps 107-115.

Royal Commission on Environmental Pollution Eleventh Report. 'Managing Waste: The Duty and Care', HMSO, December 1985.

Stegmann, R. 'Grundlagen der Deponieentgasung - Basisinformationen uber die Enstehung von Deponiegas'. Europaisches Deponiegas Forum. Munich 1986.

Winlow, A. 'Review of Landfill Gas Field Projects: Yorkshire Brick Company'. Energy from Landfill Gas. Proc. Joint UK/US D. En. Conf., Solihull, 28-31 October 1986. pps 237-249.

Table 1
Gas Exploitation Schemes

Site	Location	Waste in Place (metric tonnes)	Gas Quantity ($m^3.hr^{-1}$)	Depth of Site (m)	Specific Gas Yield ($kWm^{-2}.t^{-1}$)	Usage
Stewartby	Beds	2.0×10^6	500	22	104.9	Generation, brick kilns
Aveley	Essex	3.0×10^6	3500	25	386.3	Boilers
Norman Work	Cambs	0.3×10^6	85	12	163.09	Cement kilns
Otterspool	Merseyside	1.2×10^6	3350	10	160.0	Generation
Bidston Moss	Merseyside	2.3×10^6	934	16	167.3	Boiler firing
Stone	Kent	5.5×10^6	4400	30	424.5	Cement kiln
Azusa	California	4.1×10^6	5300	40	252	Boiler firing
Scholl Canyon	California	4.3×10^6	2360	49	74.9	Generation
Cinnaminson	N. Jersey	2.5×10^6	1180	18	230	Steel plant
Spillepeng	Sweden	1.0×10^6	350	20	232	Boilers, CHP

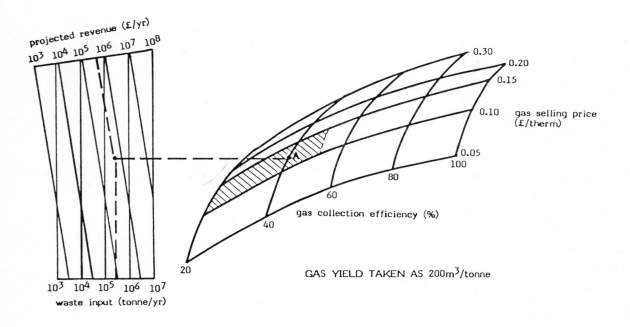

Fig 1   Nomogram for assessing likely revenue from energy sales derived from landfill gas utilization

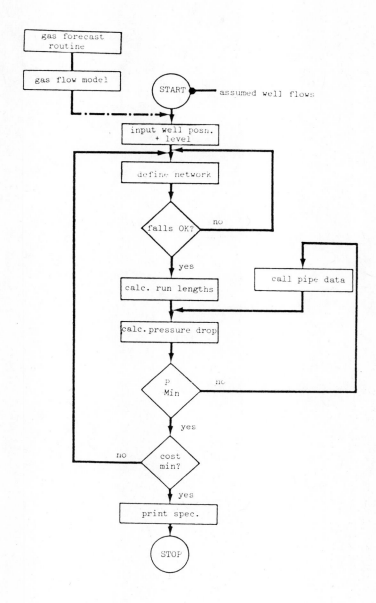

Fig 2 Logic diagram for landfill gas scheme integrated simulation and design

C01/88

Straw as a fuel

M C THOMPSON
Bedford Estates, Woburn

WHY USE STRAW AS A FUEL?

1.   It is a renewable resource.
2.   It has nil or negative value when lying in the field in areas where cereal cropping is concentrated and large scale.
3.   It will have to be disposed of in some way other than burning in the field within the foreseeable future and incorporation into the soil is not an easy solution.

WHY ONE SHOULD NOT USE STRAW AS A FUEL

1.   Straw is an inconvenient material to handle
(a)   it has to be baled
(b)   it has to be kept dry
(c)   it is a variable and unpredictable material to extract from any bale and to meter accurately via automated machinery
(d)   it is abrasive on machinery and can be very dusty
(e)   it is very expensive to handle and transport except in the near locality of production
(f)   it is a very tedious material to compress into pellets or cubes, i.e. the form in which it can easily be metered and easily supplied to a boiler or transported economically
(g)   unless great care is taken the costs of handling and processing straw can approach £100 per tonne and at that price one is competing with coal and whole grain as alternative fuels.

WHY WE CHOSE STRAW AS A FUEL AT WOBURN

1.   We grow 2000 acres of cereals and only use some 600 acres of straw for livestock.
2.   We wish to reduce our need to either burn, or incorporate, straw in the field for many reasons.
3.   We regard wood as a very expensive fuel when one allows for all the handling and storage which is required.
4.   We had three boilers which needed replacing and we had a fuel bill which was getting out of hand.
5.   We could see a potential for saving £20 000 per annum on expenditure on oil, gas and electricity.

THE PLANT AT WOBURN

The plant at Woburn is essentially a new primary heating circuit installed underground and made of preinsulated steel pipe, heated by a 2 1/2 million B.th.U. per hour Passat boiler. Three heat exchangers then act as heat transfer units to the secondary (existing) heating units in three separate blocks of historic buildings. The primary loop runs at 110 degrees centigrade under pressure.

The traditional cast iron pipework and radiators in the historic building are then not affected by the higher temperatures and pressures of the primary circuit.

The straw handling operation is the key to success or failure and great efforts were made to keep things simple and low power demanding.

Straw is handled in 4ft x 4ft (1.2 x 1.2m) round bales with non-specialised farm machinery and is delivered on a large trailer to the boiler twice per day from the nearby farm.

The straw grater is the key to the system and is a slow working low power requirement machine which teases wisps of straw out of the bale which are then carried by augers into the boiler.

The straw grater consists of a two stage conveyor holding 15 or 16 bales. One stage is a holding section onto which bales are very simply loaded with a farm tractor mounted loader. The conveyor in the base of this stage transports the bales to the shredding section under the control of photocells indicating the presence or absence of bales.

The shredding or grater section of the conveyor is the key to the whole system. The conveyor carries bales to the shredding mechanism very, very slowly under the control of an adjustable interval controlling switch. It is this interval control, with a usual setting of three seconds 'on' and twelve seconds 'off', which controls the feed rate of shredded straw to the boiler. It is the adjustment of these timing intervals which need fairly frequent attention by a boilerman.

The grater or shredder is an extremely simple device with a low power requirement which is expected to tease out wisps of straw from bales of straw which may vary from:

(a) extremely brittle, dusty, over ripe and very dry (10 per cent moisture) Wheat straw to

(b) long, waxy, non brittle and damp Winter Barley straw with every conceivable variant between these extremes.

Clearly this grater or shredder has an improbable task to perform and therefore needs fairly frequent assistance in the form of adjustments of the timing intervals on the conveyor.

The boiler is a three pass system with two sets of boiler tubes with automated tube cleaners incorporated.

The fire box is contained within ventilating silica fire blocks and is surprisingly small.

The contents of the fire box are probably about two barrowfulls at any one time and thus there are no substantial reserves of heat in the fire. The boiler has a constant feed and burn rate, but will be extinguished when there is nil heat demand and will relight on renewed heat demand.

This is a fundamentally different design from the 'whole bale' feeding system seen on other straw burning boilers.

Our choice of this more complicated system was based on the safety problems of managing a large whole bale system when a high pressure system is in use and where demand can fluctuate dramatically.

OUTLAY AND EXPERIENCES TO DATE

The whole installation has cost £150 000 but it is vital to remember that:

(a) three boilers needed replacing (£60 000)

(b) extra heating systems and control systems were added to the existing units and some areas not formerly heated were added to the systems.

The straw handling has been simple and virtually trouble free, but the accurate metering of the straw feed to the boiler is more difficult to maintain than we had hoped.

We now have a warm historic house and a reduced fuel bill, but our estimate of total heat demand was too low and a boiler of 3.5 million B.th.U. would be an advantage. Our estimate of heat demand was, of course, based primarily upon our fuel consumption and we never used enough to be warm and comfortable. We are now somewhat spoiled!

AIMS AND PROBLEMS

The aim was to save a net £20 000 per annum on fuel bills having allowed some £7000 for extra handling and staff attendance.

The costing of the straw handling is somewhat complicated, but in essence four men are involved for four weeks dealing with straw in the fields by one method or another at a total cost of perhaps £3000. Much of this cost is independent of the absence or presence of a straw burning boiler.

Delivery of straw to the boiler is twice daily by a member of staff and that costs an extra £2000 per annum.

Boiler repairs and other ancillary costs are about £2000.

The problems to date have been largely minor irritating interruptions caused basically by our inability to maintain a stable and determinable feed rate.

Unless straw feed rates are reasonably constant the boiler can fluctuate from a clinker forming state through to an unburned carbon and low output state.

Coupled with this problem are those of sophisticated control system depending on such things as photocells which frequently get confused by dust, smoke or ash.

SUMMARY

The plant has the correct design features.

The technology of straw handling is low cost and low power requiring (as seems absolutely vital).

The technology of accurately determining feed rates of a given quantity of straw is difficult to obtain and maintain.

One therefore has to realise that we are dealing with a more labour intensive system than one would ideally like. A boiler man is really required to check the boiler almost on the hour.

The economics seem good enough and, in a farming environment, we envisage having labour available in the winter for acting as boilermen.

We could undoubtedly reduce the frequency of straw feed rate problems if we used the large rectangular section Hesston bales. However, this would necessitate the use of expensive and high power requirement field machinery and thus increase the cost of handling the straw.

In short the system is exciting and has lots of potential but one does have to realize that the system can never be as automatic or clean as an oil or gas boiler.

C15/88

Profit from waste materials

B C D KERMODE, BCE, CEng, FICE, FIHT and **C WELLS**, CEng, MIMechE, MICE, MIHT, MInstWM
East Sussex County Council, Lewes, East Sussex

Considerable amounts of energy are locked up in the waste materials that society throws away and if this could be recovered economically the Nation's dependence on fossil fuels would be reduced. Over the last eight years such a process has been developed at Eastbourne in East Sussex and, as a result of its success, new plants producing some 50 000 tonnes of fuel pellets each year are being constructed at Hastings and the Isle of Wight.

Marketing the fuel is a key element in the success of such schemes and this has been assisted by the simultaneous development of combustion systems.

1. INTRODUCTION

During the last ten years, considerable progress has been made in the waste management field, which has encouraged the waste disposal industry to concentrate on the development of a more effective waste disposal strategy, with particular emphasis on the conservation of basic materials and energy. There is a considerable amount of energy in our waste materials and its economic extraction would contribute significantly to the overall energy balance. Selected waste, when treated, has considerable potential as a fuel and even the residue can be put to a useful purpose.

In the United Kingdom a total of at least 55m tonnes of solid waste is generated each year. Just over 50% is produced by industry, the remainder coming from households and commercial premises. In addition, mining, quarrying, power stations, building sites etc., produce a further 125m tonnes annually.

The potential of waste as a supplementary energy source can be clearly established if the composition and calorific value of waste are related to a coal equivalent; waste has a calorific value of about one third that of coal. (The calorific value of coal being 21 000-28 000 kJ/kg). Table 1a sets out a typical constitution of municipal waste with the relevant calorific values. The composition of municipal waste has changed over recent years, due to the reduction in the use of solid fuels and the increased use of convenience foods, resulting in a gradual increase in calorific values of municipal waste.

The world's fossil fuel reserves are diminishing year by year and our waste disposal costs are rising rapidly, so now is the time for the Engineering profession to tackle the situation by extracting profitable fractions from the waste stream to reduce overall waste disposal costs.

Table 1a Typical Composition of Municipal Waste

Composition	% by weight	Average calorific value as received (kJ/kg)
Fine Dust (- 20mm)	12	9,600
Paper	29	14,600
Vegetable	24	6,700
Metals	8	Nil
Glass	10	Nil
Rag	4	16,300
Plastic	7	37,000
Unclassified (wood, shoes etc)	6	17,600

The production of pelletised fuel from waste provides an opportunity to utilise cheap and useful energy from our waste materials.

The essential criteria for a profitable Waste Derived Fuel (WDF) project are that:-

a) proven technology is adopted;

b) finance is secured;

c) there is the political will to proceed;

d) the commercial and economic viability of the project is sound.

2. TOWARDS POSITIVE RECYCLING

Selected waste materials can produce a profit if they are recycled and any method which can achieve an environmental gain must be the aim of the waste management profession. Landfill has for a long time been accepted as the cheapest method of disposal, but as we move towards the 21st Century it is becoming increasingly difficult to find suitable sites adjacent to the densely populated areas which generate largest quantities of solid waste. Also, landfill voids are becoming scarce due to the completion of easier and more acceptable sites and the increasing standards demanded on geological, hydrological, planning and environmental grounds, thus causing associated high engineering and infrastructure costs. The only certainty is that the trend will be for disposal costs to steadily increase faster than general inflation, which makes it essential to utilise all suitable waste to produce an income with profit.

In the United Kingdom, approximately 30 million tonnes of solid waste are handled by Waste Disposal Authorities each year from households, shops, offices and factories. The average calorific value for United Kingdom Municipal waste is about 11 000 kJ/kg, while EEC waste varies between 6700-9400 kJ/kg. Compared with industrial coal (21 000-28 000 kJ/kg), the energy potential of municipal waste in the United Kingdom is equivalent to 7-10 million tonnes of coal per year. A tentative estimate of the combustible proportion of commercial/industrial waste, would indicate some 10 million tonnes/year, with an approximate calorific value of 21 000 kJ/kg and having an equivalent value of 4-8 million tonnes of coal per year. Although 15m tonnes of waste/coal equivalent appears to be a small contribution towards our energy needs, it is 14% of the coal produced in the United Kingdom in 1986.

The term 'resource recovery' includes three basic functions, which are: - material recycling; material conversion and energy recovery. When East Sussex County Council considered a recycling policy in 1974, it soon became clear that recycling schemes, on their own, failed on cost grounds due to uncertain markets and fluctuating income. This, coupled with the ever increasing cost of conventional methods of waste disposal and the continued rise in price and shortage of fossil fuels, pointed the way to concentrate on the role of waste as an energy source for the future.

At the same time, the research work carried out at Warren Spring Laboratory, together with some overseas studies, encouraged the Department of the Environment and several other County Councils to concentrate on more positive recycling processes with an emphasis on energy from waste. This determined approach has led to the construction of several waste derived fuel plants in this country; some are listed in Table 2.

Experience already gained confirms that WDF has an important role to play in the future.

The waste derived fuel process has many advantages because: -

a) The process is simple and robust;
b) The fuel has a stable calorific value at each plant and can be mixed with coal as a supplementary fuel;
c) The fuel can be produced to a uniform standard and density, it can therefore be easily handled and stored;
d) Due to the reduction process, transportation costs are reduced;
e) Less land is required for landfill;
f) Fine screenings are being developed as a growing media;
g) The principle of waste recycling is advanced;
h) Existing fossil fuels are preserved.

It is a positive and profit-earning recycling method. In general the process involves the separation of the lighter combustible elements of waste from the heavy fraction by screening, shredding, classifying, drying and ultimately, pelletization.

This paper will concentrate on the work carried out by East Sussex County Council in the development of the WDF production, combustion technology and marketing.

3. THE EASTBOURNE EXPERIENCE

The development of the Eastbourne WDF process started from the experimental work carried out at the testing laboratory of Buhler-Bros., at Uzwil, Switzerland. Lengthy and extensive testing of the pulverising, classifying and pelletization techniques were conducted. These tests resulted in the design and manufacture of the new processing machinery which was installed at Eastbourne as a full scale proving plant. The plant is based on a dry recovery process and has a maximum throughput of 10 tonnes of waste per hour. It has been in operation since 1979, initially as a joint venture with industry but, in April 1982, East Sussex County Council took over the complete operation on a commercial basis and manufactured the fuel under the trade name 'Easiburn'. Since then, the fuel has aroused great interest in both industry and commerce; sales are progressing well.

The plant currently treats some 20 000 tonnes of municipal and suitable trade waste each year, producing about 4000-5000 tonnes of fuel pellets. In addition, ferrous metals and fines (a compost material suitable as a soil conditioner), are extracted from the waste, further reducing the residue which requires ultimate disposal. Figure 1 shows a flow diagram and Table 3 is an Average Fuel Specification.

The process is in nine stages: - reception; primary milling; screening; classification; secondary milling; drying; pelletization; cooling and delivery.

To describe these in more detail: -

a) Waste material, delivered mainly in local authority collection vehicles, is discharged into a hopper which has sufficient capacity to store up to a day's input of 100 tonnes;

b) The waste is transferred, by an overhead grab, from the hopper to conveyors which feed the material to the primary mills, where it is reduced in size to a dimension of 100-125mm;

Table 3   Average fuel specification at Eastbourne Waste Derived Fuel Plant

Fuel Pellets analysis:

Bulk Density	(as received)	600kg/m^3
Moisture content of sample	(as received)	9.6% w/w
Ash content of sample	(as received)	13.0% w/w
Volatile matter content of sample	(as received)	68.3% w/w
Gross calorific value of sample	(as received)	17,910 kJ/kg
		(4,280 kcal/kg)
		(7,700 Btu/lb)
Ash content	(dry basis)	14.4% w/w
Volatile matter content	(dry basis)	75.5% w/w
Gross calorific value	(dry basis)	19,820 kJ/kg
		(4,740 kcal/kg)
		(8,520 Btu/lb)
Volatile matter content	(dry ash-free basis)	88.2% w/w
Gross calorific value	(dry ash-free basis)	23,150 kJ/kg
		(5,520 kcal/kg)
		(9,960 Btu/lb)
Chlorine content	(as received)	0.5%
Sulphur content	(as received)	0.16%

Ash analysis:

Ash fusion tests in accordance with BS.1016: Part 15 (oxidising atmosphere)

Initial Deformation Temperature	1080°C
Hemisphere Temperature	1110°C
Flow Temperature	1140°C

c)   The pulverised product is then passsed through a rotary screen where the fine fraction of minus 10mm is removed;

d)   The remaining waste is fed into the air - classifier, where the lighter cellulosic and organic material, (which forms the fuel fraction), is separated from the heavier rejected waste by a controlled air stream;

e)   The fuel fraction is removed from the top of the classifier and is blown into the secondary mill where it is further reduced in size to less than 40mm;

f)   To achieve the optimum moisture content for pelletization, the fuel fraction is dried to a maximum temperature of 460°C by a natural gas fired drying system;

g)   The material is then conveyed along a pneumatic line to the pelletiser, where it is extruded through a 20mm die to produce fuel pellets about 50mm long;

h)   The pellets are then air cooled before being transferred to the delivery system.

To appreciate the change which takes place in the WDF process, it is important to study the mass balance of materials before and after treatment.

Figure 2 shows a diagrammatic flow line of the mass balance of materials through the stages of treatment.   This should be compared with the original composition of waste as shown in Table 1b.

The balance of energy is a most important aspect of any synthetic fuel process and has been monitored and gradually improved over the last 8 years.   In general, it has been

found that the energy potential of pellets from 1 tonne of waste is about 15 times the energy consumed in the production process.

A great deal of design and operational experience has been gained during the past 8 years, all of which will be incorporated in the design and operation of new plants, ensuring that well established and proven techniques are adopted.

Table 1b   Composition of Eastbourne's Municipal Waste

Composition	% by weight	Average calorific value as received (kJ/kg)
Fine Dust (- 20mm)	3	9,600
Paper	35	14,600
Vegetable	26	6,700
Metals	8	Nil
Glass	14	Nil
Rag	3	16,300
Plastic	7	37,000
Unclassified (wood, shoes etc)	4	17,600

A brief summary of the development work which has been carried out since 1979 is as follows: -

1.   Process equipment reduced to a minimum to achieve product requirements;

2.   Mechanical handling elements streamlined and power consumption reduced;

3. Primary hammer mills converted to flails to improve efficiency, reduce operational and maintenance costs;

4. Knife Cutter replaced with purpose designed secondary mill to reduce costs;

5. Modification to Rotary Screen to improve separation efficiency and throughput;

6. Drying system re-designed to improve efficiency and reduce costs;

7. Improved pellet die design to achieve reduction in costs and longer wearing life.

4. DEVELOPMENT OF WDF PRODUCTION

Since the plant at Eastbourne started producing fuel pellets in 1979, a large number of enquiries have been received from British Local Authorities, overseas governments and large industrial companies all have shown considerable interest in the process and many have visited the Plant.

In view of this the County Council decided, in 1984, to form a private company (East Sussex Enterprises Ltd), to act as consultants in this and other areas of waste management. Recently, more positive interest has been shown both by authorities and industry which has led to the design and construction of two new WDF plants located on the Isle of Wight and at Hastings. The combined plants will treat some 165 000 tonnes of waste/year and produce about 50 000 tonnes of fuel/year. This is a major step forward in the advancement of WDF technology and should establish the role of waste as an energy source for the future.

The Isle of Wight plant will treat some 65 000 tonnes/year of waste and produce 20 000 tonnes/year of pellet fuel. The decision by the IOWCC to proceed with a WDF strategy was made following a detailed investigation into alternative waste disposal methods. Their present landfill facilities are nearing completion and further acceptable landfill sites cannot be located on this beautiful island.

Construction work has already commenced and the plant is programmed to be in operation by Mid 1988.

The larger plant, to be built at Hastings, will treat 100 000 tonnes of waste/annum and produce 30 000 tonnes of fuel/year. The decision by East Sussex County Council to proceed with this plant was made following a detailed investigation which included both operational and financial appraisals over the next 22 year period. The WDF system was compared with a landfill strategy and preferred on all counts. The adoption of the WDF system will provide an established waste disposal facility, protect the Sussex countryside from the development of further expensive landfill operations in the area, achieve savings in waste disposal operations and provide a profit which can be used to reduce the increasing costs of waste disposal in the County.

Construction has commenced and the plant is programmed to be operational by Spring 1989.

Both plants will incorporate the latest technology and well proven equipment which has been developed from operational experience at our Eastbourne Plant.

5. MARKETING AND COST IMPLICATIONS

5.1 Marketing

Marketing of the fuel is a most important element in the appraisal of a project and must be fully examined to ascertain the potential markets for the fuel before proceeding further with the project. It is therefore essential that a detailed market research study is carried out to identify both prime and secondary markets, with a reserve break-even situation to ensure that all production is sold.

When it has been decided to proceed with the project, a long term programme must be established to develop a stable market strategy.

The main issues which must be considered in the marketing of any product are: -
   Product awareness
   Product credibility
   Product financial viability

The timing of the initial marketing programme should be so designed that interest in the product is maintained right up until the plant is in production.

As waste is produced continually throughout the year, the most attractive markets are in the process industry where fuel is required at a constant rate. However, to secure flexibility it has been proven to be an advantage to establish other markets with a variety of users. The markets in East Sussex cover Local Authority establishments, industry and commerce. The success of this Marketing Strategy is mainly due to the provision of a combustion consultancy service which operates in conjunction with the production plant.

5.2 Cost Implications

Before considering the construction of a WDF plant, it is essential that a detailed feasibility study is carried out into every aspect of the project and be compared with other waste disposal operations to prove that the most economic and acceptable option has been selected. Far too many feasibility studies have been carried out with insufficient information and inaccurate financial projections, which has, unfortunately, led to the rejection of the most appropriate waste disposal method, thus losing the opportunity of achieving the best value for money. The whole life costs of every option must be evaluated. A typical example is the inaccurate costing of landfill operations. It is usual for such studies to include the void costs, site preparation works and actual operations, but the long term after care requirements such as site restoration, leachate and gas control measures are often overlooked.

6. TYPICAL PLANT SPECIFICATION

As a general guide, a WDF Plant to handle and treat 80 000-100 000 tonnes/year of household waste, the statistics would be as follows:-

6.1 Process Description (See Figure 3)

Refuse will be delivered to the plant by conventional refuse collection vehicles and a variety of trade vehicles, then discharged onto an apron storage area for handling by shovel loaders.

The incoming refuse is pushed onto plate feeder conveyors and discharged into a primary screening drum. This will separate the over-size material which requires milling before proceeding to the air classifier. The remaining material is further screened to remove the fine material and then it combines with the milled product to go forward to the classifiers. The light fraction from the classifiers is dried to the required moisture content, shredded and pelletized in a twin line process before being cooled from 100°C prior to discharge and storage.

6.2 Design Parameters

It must be noted that the process design is directly dependent upon the refuse analysis and it is most essential that an accurate waste analysis is established before a more detailed study can be undertaken.

Production and costing information in this study has been based on the assumption that the operational days/year will be 250 and the operational hours/day will be 16 hours made up of two 8 hour shifts. The maintenance will be undertaken after each working day and 8 hours have been allocated.

The reception area should be sized to accommodate a maximum of one day's waste input in the event of a plant breakdown. This size can be reduced if suitable bypass arrangements can be made.

The machinery room should be designed to accommodate all the process equipment and discharge areas.

6.3 Estimated Costs

	£
Mechanical/Electrical equipment including installation	3 500 000
Civil Engineering and Building	2 200 000
Operational Costs - per annum	600 000

These costs do not include the following as these will vary for each location.

a) All transportation of pellets and residues from the site.
b) All on site vehicles, mobile plant and containers.
c) Debt charges
d) Land acquisition costs.
e) Rates
f) Disposal costs of residues from the plant.

6.4 Estimated Production and Income

The production of fuel from the plant is approximately proportional to the quantity of input material, but for a typical waste input for Southern England the following figures apply:-

Input approx 90 000 tonnes/annum.

6.5 Production

Pellets	26 100	tonnes PA
Fines	35 100	tonnes PA
Metal	4500	tonnes PA
Rejects	17 100	tonnes PA
Moisture	7200	tonnes PA

A plant of this size can be accommodated on a site area of approximately 1 hectare. No allowance has been made for areas of land required for access roads, weighbridge and vehicle cleaning facilities, office amenity accommodation or car parking.

Income is achieved from the sale of fuel, fines, scrap metal and the treatment cost. The selling price of the pellets and the treatment price paid at the gate by Waste Disposal Authorities or others have to be in balance to give an acceptable profit margin.

The most significant income is from the sale of fuel which is currently sold at between £28-£35/tonne, ex-works, which is equivalent to some 22.5p/useful therm. Easiburn has always been competitive with other fuels. The price of alternative fuels in early 1987 was as follows:-

	Pence/useful Therm
Electricity	153
Gas (Domestic/Commercial)	50.7
Gas (Contract)	47.5
Fuel Oil (10.65p/litre)	39.1
Coal	26.7
Easiburn	22.5

The fines material is sold at about £2/tonne. However, development is proceeding to refine this material for use as a fertiliser base which should increase the value. Other experiments are being conducted to convert it to compost.

Scrap metal depends upon market forces and is currently valued at £5/tonne.

For WDF to be an acceptable proposition, the treatment cost to the Waste Disposal Authority, or any organisation which has waste for disposal, must be competitive with other methods of disposal which exist in the area.

In East Sussex, the treatment cost is related to the average cost of landfill operation. The long term appraisal carried out by the County Council, mentioned earlier, indicates that a plant based on this financial parameter would produce significant financial advantages over landfill and provide profits over a long term period.

7. COMBUSTION OF WASTE DERIVED FUEL

It was realised at the outset that the future of WDF depended upon the successful development of WDF combustion; therefore this work proceeded at the same pace. A combustion support section was set up to work in liaison with the production team and users to develop WDF boiler systems. Initial work was concentrated on heating County Council buildings to achieve savings in both energy as well as waste disposal costs.

In August 1983 time expired oil fired installations at two East Sussex Colleges were replaced with 3m Btu/hr and 4m Btu/hr automatic WDF underfeed stoker shell boiler units. These have provided good service and are still fully operational.

A similar 10m Btu/hr fully automatic WDF boiler installation has just been commissioned at Brighton Polytechnic which will be using some 1000 tonnes/year of Easiburn.

Considerable savings have been achieved in the operation of these systems and in accordance with County Council policy, appropriate installations will be replaced with WDF systems in the future.

The combustion support section has provided a service to both industry and commerce on a wide range of combustion systems including fluidised bed, chain grate, rocking grate, retort stoker, gravity feed and pulverised fuel burners.

Easiburn has a very low sulphur content being only 10% of that in coal and the chlorine content is similar to industrial coals. It can therefore be used in most types of boilers without causing corrosion, fouling or pollution. Combustion temperatures are in the range of $1000^{\circ}C$ - $1100^{\circ}C$ with exhaust gas temperatures of $950^{\circ}C$. The fuel's combustion is easily controlled by primary air modulation and the resulting fast slump and rise times provide a better response to boiler load fluctuation than other solid fuels.

It has always been our policy to work in close liaison with Government Departments, particularly with Warren Spring Laboratory and the Energy Technology Support Unit of the Department of Energy, both giving valuable technical support and assistance with the development of WDF combustion.

Warren Spring Laboratory have carried out a comprehensive study of the combustion of WDF at the Eastbourne Sixth Form College which included tests on flue gas emissions. The report is being finalised and should be released in 1987. Provided that combustion is properly controlled, as outlined in the Royal Commission on Environmental Pollution 11th Report, the emissions will not represent an environmental hazard.

Although the fuel is virtually smokeless, it is not classified as such but the Department of the Environment are the regulating authority and can issue authorisation certificates for its use in smokeless zones if they are satisfied with the design and operation of the combustion system.

As part of our commitment to the protection of the environment, we will continue to monitor the fuel and offer a combustion technology service so that our customers may be assured of the quality of our fuel at all times.

8. FUTURE PROFITS AND PROSPECTS

We the authors advise that before proceeding with a WDF project, the overriding criteria which must be satisfied are: -

a) Proven technology is adopted.

b) Finance is secured.

c) There is the political will to proceed.

d) The commercial and economic viability of the project has been assessed.

All these factors are inter-dependent and if any one should fail the project will be unsuccessful.

As we move toward the 21st Century it will become increasingly difficult to find suitable landfill sites, particularly adjacent to urban areas and with the rising costs of void spaces, transport and higher standards for site preparation, operation and after care, localised facilities for treating waste with maximum reclamation will be required.

A preliminary appraisal indicates that, in the UK, currently some 5 million tonnes per annum of waste could be treated to produce WDF thereby reducing the pressure on the need to establish additional landfill facilities.

It should also be borne in mind that with the continuing changes in our living standards the amount of refuse produced will rise.

For example, compared with this country, the United States of America produces up to twice the amount of refuse per head. As these quantities increase the WDF process of extracting energy from waste will become of even greater importance.

Engineering profit from waste will only happen if Engineers with sound commercial and management ability are prepared to work with determination and enthusiasm towards the achievement of both financial and environmental profits from our waste materials.

Table 2   Some UK Waste Derived Fuel Plants

Plant	Treatment Method	Reclaimed Materials	Status
Eastbourne East Sussex County Council	Primary shredding, screening, classification, secondary shredding, pelletisation	Waste Derived Fuel Pellets Fines Ferrous metals	Operational since 1979
Byker Newcastle City Council	Primary shredding, screening, classification, secondary shredding, pelletisation	Waste Derived Fuel Pellets Ferrous metals	Operational since 1980
Doncaster	Screening, classification, shredding, pelletisation	Waste Derived Fuel Pellets Ferrous metals Fibre Fines	For sale (commissioned 1980)
Govan Glasgow City Council	Primary shredding, screening, classification, secondary shredding, pelletisation	Waste Derived Fuel Pellets	Operational since 1983
Castle Bromwich City of Birmingham	Primary shredding, screening, classification, secondary shredding, pre-densification pelletisation	Waste Derived Fuel Pellets Ferrous metals	Operational since 1985
Huyton Merseyside WDF Ltd	Primary shredding, screening, classification, secondary shredding, pre-densification pelletisation	Waste Derived Fuel Pellets Ferrous metals	Operational since 1986
Isle of Wight IOW County Council	Screening, primary shredding, classification, secondary shredding, pelletisation	Waste Derived Fuel Pellets Fines Ferrous metals	Commissioning 1988
Pebsham, Hastings East Sussex County Council	Screening, primary shredding, classification, secondary shredding, pelletisation	Waste Derived Fuel Pellets Fines Ferrous metals	Commissioning 1989

ACKNOWLEDGMENTS

Buhler Bros, Uzwil, Switzerland

Buhler - Miag (England) Ltd,
(Plant Construction)

Department of Energy - ETSU

Department of Trade and Industry -
Warren Spring Laboratory

East Sussex Enterprises Ltd

'The Challenge of Waste Disposal',
The County Surveyors Society, 1983

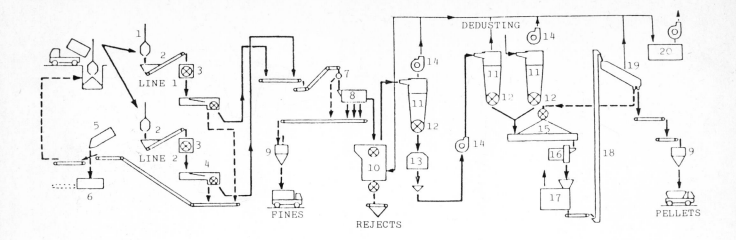

1	Grab	6	Metal Press	11	Cyclone	16	Pellet Mill
2	Slat Conveyors	7	Change-over Flap	12	Air Lock	17	Cooler
3	Primary Mills	8	Screening Drum	13	Secondary Mill	18	Bucket Elevator
4	Metal Extractors	9	Surge Hopper	14	Fan	19	Throw Sieve
5	Overband Magnet	10	Air Classifier	15	Drying Unit	20	American Air Filter

Fig 1   Eastbourne waste derived fuel plant flow diagram

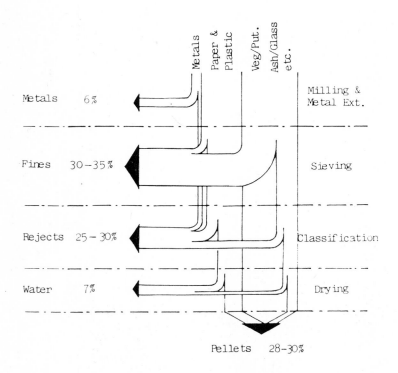

Fig 2   Material mass balance

Domestic & Commercial Waste

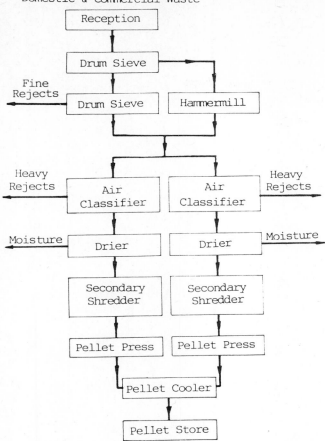

Fig 3　Proposed schematic flowline, 80 000 — 100 000 tonnes per annum

Fig 4　Hopper and 2 m Btu/h waste derived fuel (WDF) boiler at Eastbourne Sixth Form College

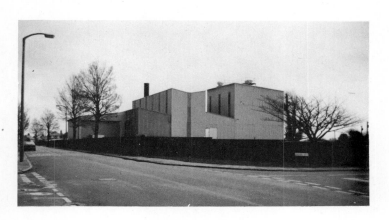

Fig 5　Eastbourne WDF plant

Refuse derived fuel – improved profitability by composting the fines residue

E I STENTIFORD, MA, MSc, CEng, MIMechE, S KELLING, BSc and J L ADAMS, BSc
Department of Civil Engineering, The University of Leeds

SYNOPSIS   A 12-month study showed that co-composting of fines residues from refuse-derived fuel processing with sewage sludge is a technically feasible operation that can be economically advantageous when sanitary landfill disposal costs are high.

1   INTRODUCTION

The major solid waste disposal problem facing us today is related to domestic refuse. Few of specific components of domestic refuse in themselves pose an intrinisic disposal problem: the difficulty is associated with the shear quantity of material. In the UK approximately 29×10^6 tonnes of refuse are disposed of by local authorities every year (1), approximately 80% of which ends up in sanitary landfills.

A high proportion of domestic refuse is recoverable but the economics of recovery are such that the magnetic separation of ferrous metals is the only commonly used recycling route. It is interesting to group together some of the components of refuse rather than to consider specific items. On this basis we find that approximately two thirds can be classed as combustibles and putrescible. The rapid rise in oil prices which occurred in recent years has directed many bodies to examine this combustible fraction in order to assess its potential as an alternative fuel.

Four main energy recovery routes have been studied in some detail: incineration with heat recovery, pyrolysis, methane production through anaerobic digestion, and the production of refuse derived fuels (RDF). Of these four it is probably RDF which has attracted most funding and interest as it was seen as a direct competitor for coal, being able to utilise existing furnace systems. Although the calorific value of pelletised RDF is less than coal (typically 16 MJ/kg compared to 27 for coal) at the right market price it is seen as a viable commercial alternative (2).

The variability of the refuse feedstock due to seasonal changes, social practices and different living standards is reflected in the quality of the RDF. This variability also affects the quantities of reject material generated at RDF plants. The fines reject stream, which has a high proportion of organic material, typically constitutes around 30% of the total tonnage being processed. This percentage changes due to the variables mentioned previously and to the type of RDF production system employed.

Current practice with the fines reject material is to dispose of it to landfill. How-ever, it has been identified as having potential for reuse, possibly in the form of compost. In order to assess this potential Leeds University, funded by the Department of the Environment, carried out a 12 month pilot study. This study was designed primarily to determine the composting properties of the material but was also constrained by consideration of the economic feasibility of any additional materials processing which would be necessary.

Figure 1 shows schematically some of the processes involved in producing RDF. Alongside the fuel stream a possible composting sequence is shown taking the fines rejects from the trommel screen. The compost route does not utilise all the fines since to produce a good final product the compost is often screened using 8-12 mm mesh. The incoming fines represent the throughput from a screen whose mesh size might range from 20 to 40 mm, depending on the design philosophy of the fuel stream. Consequently there will be a certain proportion of oversize rejects from the compost screen which have to be landfilled.

2   COMPOSTING – GENERAL

For many thousands of years composting in various forms has been practiced by the farming community to reuse organic wastes. During the past 50 years the process has been put on a far more scientific basis as our understanding improved. This has been evidenced by the many different commercial systems which have been, and in many cases still are, widely used (3).

The basic principle of composting is to provide optimal conditions for the aerobic biodegradation of the organic solids. This requires certain characteristics with respect to: moisture content (initial value 55-65% for refuse based mixtures), particle size, free air space and carbon/nitrogen ratio (initial value 25-40 for refuse based mixtures). These are considered for several wastes by Haug (4), although it should be realised that each new combination of materials might require different operating conditions. The aerobic breakdown of organic solids is an exothermic process and this together with the insulating properties of the composting mass restricts the heat loss to the environment producing an increase in temperature. This increase in temperature increases the activity of the microorganisms and hence the rate of heat production. This activity is greatest in the range 55-60°C (5), but is severely restricted above 65°C. Ideally a composting plant should maintain an operating temperature around 55°C which maximises activity and hence reduces the processing time required to stabilise the organic waste. The shorter the stabilisation time, the smaller the reactor for a specific throughput and hence the lower the cost.

The materials deposited in the typical dustbin cover a wide range and have differing degrees of bacterial contamination. One of the common indicators of faecal contamination, Escherichia coli (E.coli) can be present in numbers as high as 10^7 organisms/g wet material. Although we may not be certain as to the specific source of these organisms it is desirable that their numbers be considerably reduced if we require a marketable end product. Fortunately by maintaining the correct operating conditions it is possible to reduce these numbers to less than 10^2 organisms/g which is thought to be a reasonable level of sanitisation. In many cases government regulations stipulate a minimum exposure of the material for 3 days at 55°C, the inactivation of these organisms being temperature and exposure time dependent.

Until recently in order to achieve close control of operating conditions expensive reactor based systems were the only viable high rate processes. However, work carried out in the United States on sewage sludge/woodchip mixtures opened up new low cost possibilities. This work was extended to refuse/sludge mixtures in the UK some 5 years ago (6).

3   FINES COMPOSTING

The work reported in this paper relates to the fines rejects from the Grimsby RDF plant, but confirmation of some of the results has been made with fines from the Castle Bromwich plant.

For a fines composting plant to be a practical proposition its costs must not represent a major part of the RDF plants costs. Consequently the choice is restricted to low cost systems which can maintain close control of the operating conditions. There are few such systems available and the one which best satisfies the conditions is the aerated static pile. It was this static pile system, employing temperature feedback control, which was used in this study. A section through a typical pile used is shown in Figure 2 with the air being supplied through perforated pipe at a rate depending on the stage of the process.

Table 1 shows the range and mean of some of the parameters most relevant to the composting process. The research programme at Leeds examined different mixtures of fines, sewage sludge, bulking agent and water. The process performance differed in each case, but this was often related to the changing quality of the fines rather than the mixture being used. Typically, using temperature feedback control, the mean control temperature (55-60°C) in the pile core was maintained for around 4 weeks. At the end of this period there was insufficient heat generated by the biodegradation to hold the control temperature.

Figure 3 shows the variation of temperature with time for one of the experimental runs, which for the most part was typical of this type of material. This particular example was used to illustrate the effect on the pile temperatures of repositioning the control probe.

At the end of the 4 week rapid bio-oxidation stage the compost is generally stored in non-aerated piles for around 4 months, if it is intended for general purpose use. Without this period of maturation the compost can inhibit certain plant functions. The nature of this inhibition is not fully understood nor are the processes which take place during maturation to improve the all round qualities of the compost. Table 2 shows some of the characteristics of the compost at the end of the aeration phase and at the end of maturation. A comparison with Table 1 shows the changes which take place during composting.

In a properly run aerated static pile system the heat generated by the breakdown of the volatile solids is used to evaporate moisture. Although an initial moisture content in the 55-65% range is ideal, at the end of the aeration phase a value around 40% is desirable to enable effective screening of the compost. The N, P and K value of the material should change little although a certain amount of nitrogen is lost as ammonia. The sanitisation effect of the process is demonstrated by the reduction in E.coli to less than 10^2cfu/gww. The microbiological analysis was only carried out for a few piles to confirm previously reported findings (7).

4   PRODUCT QUALITY AND USE

Limited plant growth trials with the mature fines compost for the most part confirmed previous findings with refuse based materials. Although the results were variable the general conclusions were that the material performed as well as a good topsoil and often exceeded the performance of commercial composts. An example of this using tomatoes is given in Figure 4 where the fines compost (shown as 'Doncaster' compost) outperformed both the high pH (6.5 - 7) and low pH (5.5 - 6) control composts. The two mixes shown represented a 1:1 mixture by volume of fines compost and the control and they performed similarly to the fines compost.

On the practical side with the tonnages involved in a fines composting operation it is unlikely that the total output will be used in tomato growing. It is necessary to establish larger markets which require compost over a far greater part of the year. One such possible market is land reclamation linked to industries such as mining, which create large areas of land devoid of growing medium and on which compost could be used for a high proportion of the year. If sales are tied into crops such as tomatoes then the compost will only be required for about 3 months of the year necessitating expensive storage for the remaining 9 months. At this point in time no studies have been carried out to determine potential market size.

One of the major difficulties currently being faced by existing RDF plants is the lack of a large constant demand market. To add a composting operation to the RDF facility without some very firm markets of this type would seem at best to be foolhardy.

5 FINES COMPOSTING - PROFIT OR LOSS?

It is unfortunate that in the minds of many waste disposal authorities the word composting is linked inexorably with profit. In some cases it might be possible to achieve this but even with one of the lowest cost controlled processes i.e. the aerated static pile, it is generally only possible to reduce disposal costs, rather than make an operating profit. In order to demonstrate some of the financial aspects of a fines composting operation some estimated cost figures are presented in Table 3 for a 50 tonne/day plant (12000 tonnes/yr). This would take the fines from an RDF plant processing around 150 tonnes of refuse/day. The costs are for treatment and disposal only, not collection, so the assumption is that the refuse arrives at zero cost to the plant.

The costs have been prepared on the assumption that the composting plant will operate alongside the RDF plant thus reducing the need for excess staffing and other increased costs appropriate to an entirely separate unit.

If we assume a compost selling price of £10/tonne (based on an ex-works price for similar material in bulk) then in order for the plant to break even or make a "profit", related to all the refuse going along the landfill disposal route, the following relationship must hold (from Table 3).

$$12 \text{ (LDR)} \geq 131.5 + 3.6 \text{ (LDR)} - 48$$

i.e. the landfill disposal rate (LDR) $\geq$ £9.95/tonne.

There are areas in the UK where disposal costs of this order exist making the additional composting operation economically viable. It is important to note that the reject material from the composting plant will not present a vermin problem at the landfill site since the organic matter it contains would be biologically stable. However, this has not been included in the economic equation.

At the end of the day the profitability on paper has very little meaning without the most important ingredient, an assured market for the product. It is essential that marketing of the compost begins long before the plant is completed. The majority of composting installations which have closed down in Europe in recent years have done so because of the lack of an established market.

6 ACKNOWLEDGEMENTS

The research reported in this paper was funded by the Department of the Environment under contract number PECD 7/10/81 - 130/ 84.

7 REFERENCES

(1) Digest of Environmental Pollution and Water statistics, No. 9 (1986), Department of the Environment, HMSO.

(2) Jackson, D.V. and Tron, A.R. (1985). Energy from Wastes. International Journal of Ambient Energy, Vol. 6, No. 1, pp.31-44.

(3) Stentiford, E.I. (1986). Recent Developments in Composting, In: "Compost Production Quality and Use", published by Elsevier Applied Science.

(4) Haug, R.T. (1980). "Compost Engineering - Principles and Practice", published by Ann Arbor Science, Michigan, USA.

(5) McKinley, V.L., Vestal, J.R. and Eralp, A.E. (1985). Microbial Activity in Composting, Biocycle, 26, 7, pp. 47-50.

(6) Stentiford, E.I., Mara, D.D. and Taylor, P.L. (1985). "Froced Aeration Composting of Domestic Refuse and Sewage Sludge in Static Piles", In: Composting of Agricultural and Other Wastes, edited by J.K.R. Gasser, Elsevier Applied Science, pp.42-54, 1985.

(7) Pereira-Neto, J.T., Stentiford, E.I. and Smith, D.V. (1986). "Survival of Faecal Indicator Micro-organisms in Refuse/Sludge Composting Using the Aerated Static Pile System", Waste Management and Research, 4, pp. 397-406.

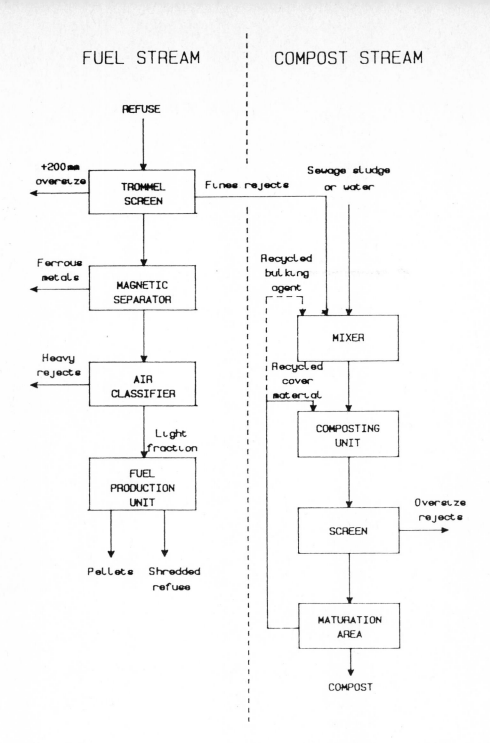

FUEL STREAM | COMPOST STREAM

Fig 1   Schematic of a composting unit running in parallel with a refuse
derived fuel plant

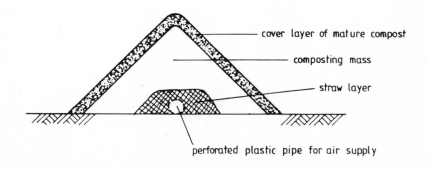

cover layer of mature compost

composting mass

straw layer

perforated plastic pipe for air supply

Fig 2   Cross-section of a typical aerated static pile

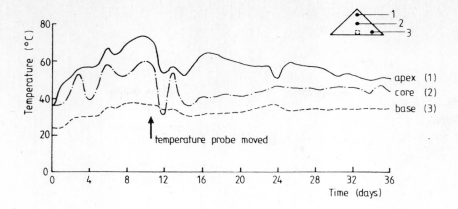

Fig 3 Temperature/time profile for a typical compost pile, showing the effect of moving the temperature control probe

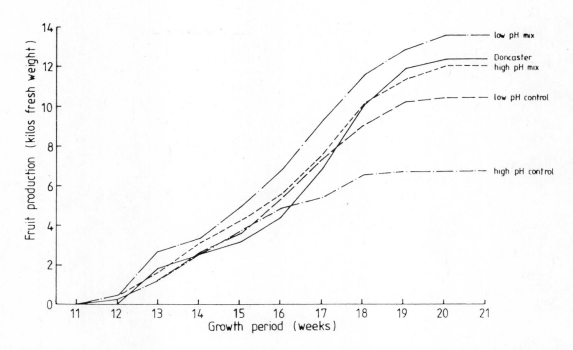

Fig 4 Tomato production with different composts ('Doncaster' = fines compost)

Table 1 Refuse fines and sewage sludge characteristics

Parameter	Refuse Range	Mean	Sludge Range	Mean	Mixture Range	Mean
pH	5–6.6	5.6	5.8–7.5	6.4	5.1–5.9	5.4
Moisture (%WW)	35–40	38	93.7–96.7	95.8	59–63	60.5
Volatile Solids (%DM)	35–75.9	60.2	66.6–89.0	76.1	59–65.3	61.9
Bulk Density (kg.m^{-3})	150–191	171	–	–	240–290	265
Nitrogen (%DM)	0.76–1.6	1.14	3.04–7.05	5.55	0.99–1.01	1.00
Phosphorus (%DM)	0.25–0.28	0.27	1.52–2.02	1.77	–	0.47
Potassium (%DM)	0.36–0.99	0.62	0.49–0.89	0.65		
E.coli (cfu/gww)	–	–	–	–	–	4×10^7

Note: %WW = percentage of the weight
%DM = percentage of dry matter
cfu/gww = colony forming units per gramme wet weight

Table 2   Compost characteristics based on all the refuse/sludge
           mixtures used in aerated static piles

	Day 30		4 months mature	
Parameter	Range	Mean	Range	mean
pH	7.1-8.2	7.8	6.9-7.6	7.3
Moisture (%WW)	36.5-52.9	45.1	39.8-49.3	43.3
Volatile Solids (%DM)	35.2-49.1	41.4	29.7-36.6	32.3
Bulk Density (kg. m^{-3})	249-294	276	325-402	371
Nitrogen (%DM)	0.87-1.21	1.00	1.06-1.22	1.10
Phosphorus (%DM)	0.43-0.73	0.56	0.54-0.69	0.61
Potassium (%DM)	0.44-0.91	0.73	0.57-0.77	0.69
E.coli (cfu/gww)	-	$<10^2$	-	$<10^2$

Note: %WW = percentage of the wet weight
        %DM = percentage of dry matter
    cfu/gww = colony forming units per gramme wet weight

Table 3   Costs for a 50 tonnes/day fines composting plant

ITEM	COSTS (£ x 10^3)

Capital

Civil (concrete work area and buildings)	190
Mechanical/Electrical front loaders	80
controllers and blowers	50
mixer	30
screens and conveyors	35

Annual

Civil (capital over 20 years)	25.5
Mechanical/Electrical (capital over 10 years)	32
Labour	36
Aeration pipe	7
Straw	3
Maintenance	16
Other (inc. contingency)	12
Total annual installation costs	131.5
Disposal of screenings rejects	3.6 LDR[1]
Sales of compost	(2) 4.8 CSP[3]

Notes: (1) LDR = Landfill disposal rate £/tonne
       (2) Based on a compost yield at 40% of the input gives 4800
           tonnes/yr.
       (3) CSP = Compost selling price £/tonne

Landfill gas extraction–vertical wells or horizontal trenches?

P FLETCHER, BSc, CChem, MRSC
Environmental Safety Centre, Harwell Laboratory, Oxfordshire

SYNOPSIS   This paper describes a project undertaken to assess the effectiveness of horizontal gas collection trenches for the abstraction of landfill gas and to compare their performance with that of vertical wells. Although rising leachate levels within the waste seriously affected the performance of both systems, the work did demonstrate that horizontal trenches may be used successfully and that in certain circumstances they have advantages over vertical wells. The choice of which system to use at a particular site, however, is very dependent on the nature of the site and the method of filling. Advantages and disadvantages of each system are discussed.

1   INTRODUCTION

By early 1987 there were eleven landfill sites in the UK where landfill gas was being commercially abstracted for its energy value. Consisting primarily of methane and carbon dioxide in the approximate ratio of 60:40, landfill gas has a calorific value approximately half that of natural gas. It may therefore be used as a replacement for fossil fuels and it has been estimated that in 1986 the total energy supplied by landfill gas in the UK was 16.5 million therms (1.7 million GJ), equivalent to 66,000 tonnes of coal(1). Most, but by no means all, commercial schemes in the UK are based at large landfill sites where there is a large energy consumer nearby. The gas is commonly used as a direct fuel replacement such as in brick or cement kilns or as a boiler fuel (paper and food manufacture). Electricity generation through the use of landfill gas powered internal combustion engines and gas turbines, however, is receiving increasing interest because at many sites there are no suitable end users for the gas within a convenient distance.

2. VERTICAL WELLS

The traditional method of extracting biogas from a landfill site, and that employed at the majority of sites where gas is commercially utilised, is via a series of vertical wells inserted into the waste. Although a system whereby vertical wells are constructed by stacking a number of perforated concrete rings as the waste is built up has been tried at some sites, this tends to be unsuccessful due to problems of uneven settlement and air ingress around them. It is now generally accepted that vertical gas extraction wells should be constructed by drilling into the waste after it has been brought up to its final level. The details of well construction tend to vary little from site to site and a typical configuration is shown in Figure 1.

Initially a borehole is drilled into the waste, usually by the shell and auger technique, almost to the base of the site or until the landfill water table is reached. The borehole has a diameter of 0.3-1.0m and for safety reasons is cased during drilling to minimise gas release. A plastic well pipe, 0.1-0.15m in diameter and perforated except for the top few metres is inserted into the drilled hole. The annulus is back filled with permeable material such as pea gravel or broken bricks and is capped with a 'plug' of impermeable material. The well is finished off with a suitable valve and monitoring points (to enable gas composition, temperature, pressure and flow rate to be determined) prior to connection with the gas collection main.

The spacing of vertical wells depends to a large extent on site specific criteria such as type of waste, density and quality of cover materials. Well locations must, therefore, generally be determined from the results of preliminary pumping trials performed on two or three wells. For most sites, however, it can be expected that each well will have a radius of influence of about 50m if the applied suction can be suitably adjusted.

3   HORIZONTAL WELLS

An alternative system of collecting landfill gas, using a series of horizontal wells (trenches) laid across the waste at one or more levels within the site, has been tried at a few sites. A potential attraction of horizontal wells is the ability to extract gas from lower levels within a site, while waste is still being deposited at higher levels, ie before the final site contours have been reached.

Horizontal wells are usually constructed by firstly excavating a trench approximately 1m deep and 1m wide across the required layer of waste. Gravel is then placed in the trench to a depth of about 0.15m prior to the insertion of a 0.15m diameter perforated pipe. Brick rubble is placed at either side of the pipe to protect it and a layer of filter material is placed over the pipe before the trench is refilled with excavated waste. A schematic cross-section through a typical horizontal well is shown in Figure 2.

4   STAIRFOOT QUARRY PROJECT

4.1 Aims

In order to assess the effectiveness of horizontal gas collection trenches for the abstraction of landfill gas and to compare their performance with that of vertical wells, Harwell undertook a monitoring programme on behalf of the Department of Energy. The work was carried out at the Stairfoot Quarry landfill site in Barnsley, South Yorkshire where gas is abstracted for use in the adjacent Yorkshire Brick Company brick kilns. This particular site was chosen because one area of the site was filled in two phases with vertical wells being installed in the first and horizontal trenches incorporated in the second phase.

4.2 Gas utilisation at the site

Stairfoot Quarry was created by the excavation of mudstones and shales for brick manufacture and the void thus formed was infilled with mainly domestic waste. There are actually three distinct areas to the quarry as shown in Figure 3. Area A was filled up to 1978 and a testing programme carried out by Harwell in 1981 revealed the potential for commercial gas abstraction for this area and the future landfill area B. A pilot plant was built and operational by mid 1983 supplying gas with an energy value of 170 therms day^{-1} to the brick kiln. The main interest however, was in the much larger area B and this is where Harwell's monitoring programme was undertaken.

4.3 Gas collection - Area B

The first phase of area B was filled with domestic and trade waste between 1982 and 1984 and ten vertical wells were installed prior to the addition of a 2m clay cap. Construction of the wells was as outlined above with each being 0.2m in diameter and between 10 and 15m deep. Perforated polyethylene pipes of 0.1m diameter were used and the annuli were filled with pea gravel. Each well was fitted with a valve and orifice plate to measure flowrates. The location of the vertical wells is shown on a plan of phase 1 in Figure 4.

Phase 2 of area B was started in May 1984. The operational plan for this part of the site was essentially to place a 2.5m layer of waste across the whole area before the emplacement of further layers. Horizontal gas collection trenches are ideal for this method of landfilling because each collection pipe may be placed across an entire layer of the site in one operation.

No gas collection trenches were put in the first two layers of waste but on completion of layer 3 a single trench (H2), 170m long was excavated across the site. A perforated, 0.15m diameter polyethylene pipe was installed in the trench and surrounded by a permeable gravel/brick infill as described above. At the same time another short trench (H1) was installed to collect gas from the flank of phase 1.

It had become apparent at this stage that leachate levels were rising in both phases of area B (see below) and that they were only just below the surface of the waste when layer 3 was completed. To avoid flooding of the gas collection trenches by this unanticipated high leachate level a spur trench was connected to the centre of H2. This trench, running NE to SW, contained 0.15m diameter perforated polypropylene (Aqua-pipe) and it was hoped that it would drain leachate from layer 3.

In case this did not occur, and layer 3 became flooded, three trenches were installed within layer 4. The first of these was a 170m extension to H1 using polyethylene pipe (Demco terrascreen). The other two trenches (H3 and H4) were constructed using a pipe made from recycled polypropylene which is a much less expensive material. All three pipes were 0.15m diameter and surrounded by brick rubble.

Two gas collection pipes were installed in layer 5 by means of specialised pipe-laying plant. Both of these were 0.15m poly-propylene pipes placed without the protection of brick rubble and were connected to the central pipe in layer 4 (i.e. H4).

Three polypropylene gas collection trenches were installed in layer 6 (H5, H6 and H7).

After completion of layers 7 and 8, into which no gas collection trenches were installed, the front of the site (south-west area) was filled. Two gas collection trenches (H8 and H9) were installed in the third layer of this area (3A).

Three additional gas collection points (H2A, H2B and H2C) were added in September 1986 and connected to the gas main replacing the now flooded H2. The gas collection system for phase 2 is summarised in Table 1 and Figure 5 shows a plan of phase 2 indicating the location of all the gas collection pipes. A cross-section through phase 2 is presented in Figure 6 to demonstrate the vertical separation of pipes.

Each collection pipe (or 'family of pipes) was connected to the gas collection main via a valve and orifice plate so that flow rates could be monitored.

4.4 Modifications to vertical well system

Although phase 1 was completed and the vertical gas extraction wells were installed prior to Harwell's monitoring programme commencing, a number of modifications had to be made during this period.

Rising leachate levels caused problems with the effective operation of the lower wells (7-10) because liquid rose almost to the top of the perforated well pipes. In an attempt to collect gas more efficiently from this area a trench was excavated along a line just south of wells 7-10. The construction methods employed were similar to those for the phase 2 horizontal trenches with polypropylene (Aqua-pipe) being used. Although good quality gas accumulated in this horizontal trench, serious problems of air ingress which occurred when suction was applied meant that the trench was never utilised.

Instead, an alternative way of overcoming the problem of high leachate levels was adopted. Alongside each of the original wells 7-10, new wells were drilled and pipes with shorter unperforated sections were installed. The length of perforated pipe above the leachate was thereby increased. It was hoped that this would be only a temporary measure and that the leachate levels could be reduced enabling the original wells to be reconnected. By the end of the monitoring period, however, this had not been achieved.

By early in 1986 it was also apparent that landfill gas was escaping from the surface of phase 1 along its NW flank. In order to prevent this, a horizontal gas collection trench (6A) was installed along this bank and connected to the gas main via a control valve and orifice plate in a manhole adjacent to well number 6.

4.5 Rising leachate levels

It was established that the problem of rising leachate levels within the site, as already discussed, was due to groundwater infiltration (2). Initially, leachate seeping from the southern end of the site was merely re-circulated by reinjecting it into the waste at the northern part of the site. This exacerbated the problem but leachate was later disposed off site by passing it to foul sewer. Throughout the monitoring period, however, there were consistently high leachate levels in phase 1, with the water table typically being only 6m below the surface of the site at well number 10. The various attempts to overcome the problems which the shallow depth of unsaturated waste presented to gas abstraction have already been described.

Despite these, very little gas was collected from the lower parts of phase 1.

Similar problems were experienced within phase 2. Horizontal trench H2 in layer 3 was covered by leachate within a few weeks of its installation and the soakaway limb did not achieve a reduction in leachate level as hoped. In fact the height of the leachate table increased further so that two of the gas collection trenches (H1 and H4) in layer 4 also became blocked. Only the most southerly trench (H3) remained free of leachate because of the gradient in the liquid level caused by groundwater entering the quarry from the north and leachate seeping out at the southern side.

4.6 Landfill gas production

Figure 7 shows the gradual increase in the total energy provided to the kilns by landfill gas and by the end of 1986 this had reached approximately 1000 therms day^{-1}. Knowing the flow rate of gas from individual wells and trenches for the particular days of monitoring, the approximate amount of energy provided by each phase may be calculated and is also shown on Figure 7. It is apparent that during the monitoring period there was a slight reduction in the rate of gas extracted from phase 1 accompanied by a gradual increase in the gas production for phase 2.

The reduction from approximately 600 therms day^{-1} down to approximately 400 therms day^{-1} for the energy value of gas from phase 1 may be explained by the problems of the rising leachate level. Virtually no gas was extracted from the four lowest wells (7, 8, 9 and 10) in this phase during 1986 despite the introduction of the shortened pipes. A slight increase in the amount of gas utilised from phase 1 did occur briefly with the intro-duction of gas collection trench 6A in June 1986. Loss of substrate and a cooling effect due to groundwater ingress probably also contributed to the reduced rate of methane production.

Gas abstraction from phase 2 commenced in May 1985 (see Table 1) and, as demonstrated by Figure 6, increased (irregularly) throughout the period of monitoring up to approximately 600 therms day^{-1} by December 1986. Only the gas collection trenches in layers 4 and 5 were being used because lower levels of waste were flooded and higher levels had not been in place long enough for gas production to have reached the rate at which extraction was worthwhile. It can be expected that much more gas will become available when higher levels of waste are utilised.

Towards the end of the monitoring period the extraction pump was working at its maximum capacity. This made it difficult to assess the full potential for gas production from the whole site because increasing the suction on one well or trench merely reduced the suction and hence amount of gas extracted from the others. A new pump having a greater capacity was installed in February 1987 to handle the increased volumes of gas which are expected to be produced when trenches H5-H9 come on stream.

4.7 Economic assessment

The total cost of the complete gas extraction system up to the end of December 1986 was approximately £150,000 with projected costs of a further £10,000 for the new pump. In December 1986 the cost of natural gas was 32p per therm, hence the savings due to reduced natural gas requirements were running at about £10,000 per month. As a significant increase in the amount of landfill gas being collected can be expected, the payback period on the total investment in gas extraction equipment will be less than 15 months.

The relative costs (£ per m of pipe) for installing the vertical wells and horizontal trenches are not directly comparable because different pipe materials were used.

A theoretical comparison of the relative costs, for the two types of system may be made however, by assuming, firstly, that the same pipe material was used throughout. The cost of installing the ten vertical wells using polypropylene well pipe would then have been £24.2 per metre compared with the cost of installing horizontal trenches of £12 per metre. Hence, using these costs, for horizontal trenches to be as economical as vertical wells, they would only need to be able to extract half as much gas per unit length. At Stairfoot Quarry however the total length of horizontal trenches was over 1500m which is 13 times more than the total 'length' of vertical well pipe. To be as cost effective as the vertical well system, the horizontal trenches therefore needed to yield six times as much gas whereas they actually only produced approximately twice as much gas.

It seems most likely, however, that more trenches than necessary have been installed in phase 2 and work done in Canada(3) has indicated that horizontal wells may be used effectively with up to 8m vertical separation.

A true assessment from the data obtained at Stairfoot is obviously difficult because of the rising leachate level which effectively prevented the use of three horizontal wells.

4.8 Summary of the findings from the Stairfoot project

Despite the need for continual modifications to the gas collection system, primarily due to rising leachate levels, the total cost for installing wells, trenches, pipelines and pumps was only approximately £150,000 giving a payback period of less than 15 months on the gas extraction equipment.

The detrimental effect of rising leachate levels on both types of landfill gas collection system was clearly demonstrated. Three of the horizontal trenches and four vertical wells were rendered inoperative due to blocking by leachate and the efficiency of the remaining vertical wells was also reduced. Overcoming these problems was easier with the horizontal trench system because gas extraction was switched to trenches in higher, unsaturated levels of waste whereas with the vertical wells it necessitated the drilling of new wells.

Care must be taken, however, in applying these findings to other sites, particularly those at the planning stage. It would be preferable to ensure that a site being considered for commercial gas abstraction is suitably engineered so that the serious problems of water ingress did not occur in the first place. The advantage of being able to use horizontal trenches in higher levels of waste, above the leachate table, would then not be apparent.

This work has shown, however, that an existing site with a similar problem of a high leachate table may be utilised for landfill gas abstraction by constructing trenches in the higher, unsaturated layers of waste.

The use of horizontal trenches in phase 2 enabled significant quantities of landfill gas to be extracted while waste was still being deposited at higher levels. Approximately 160,000 therms of energy had been provided by the gas from phase 2 up to December 1986 and there was still a further 2 months landfilling remaining. A vertical well arrangement in this part of the site would not have yielded any gas in the same period because construction of the wells could not have commenced until the landfill operation was complete.

Again, however, it is unrealistic to claim that this is a universally applicable advantage of horizontal trenches because the operational plan of depositing waste in layers across the whole of phase 2 was ideal for this system. This method of depositing waste goes against the current recommendations of working in a small area of a landfill site at any one time to allow progressive restoration(4). If phase 2 at Stairfoot had been filled in two or three stages gas abstraction by vertical wells would have been possible prior to the completion of the whole phase and progressive capping would also have been accomplished reducing the amount of rain water infiltration. The use of horizontal trenches in this case would not have been so appropriate because a lot of relatively short lengths would have been required.

The study was valuable in demonstrating that where there is an operational need to fill a site in large areas, so that its depth is built up slowly, horizontal trenches may be employed to extract gas during the operational phase.

5   CONCLUSIONS

The Stairfoot Quarry project did not provide conclusive evidence as to which particular system, vertical wells or horizontal trenches, is the most effective means of extracting landfill gas. It did, however, demonstrate some of the relative merits and drawbacks of each system and indicated that the decision about which system should be used at a particular site will depend on a number of site specific parameters. At many sites, therefore, the choice will be quite obvious e.g. a deep site which is already filled with waste will require vertical wells whereas horizontal trenches would be more suited to a shallow site covering a large area.

The advantages and disadvantages of each system are summarised in Table 2.

ACKNOWLEDGEMENTS

The work at Stairfoot Quarry was funded by the Department of Energy and the author would also like to thank Mr A Winlow of the Yorkshire Brick Company for his assistance with this project.

REFERENCES

(1) RICHARDS, K. M. Landfill gas exploitation - Demonstration schemes in the UK. Proceedings of the Energy from Landfill Gas Conference, Solihull, 28-31 October 1986.

(2) CRIMES, T. P. Land reclamation at Stairfoot Brickworks Pit: Geological Aspects, May 1980.

(3) GRAZIANI, W., CRUTCHER, A. J. Landfill gas horizontal trench collection system, Keele Valley Landfill. Proceedings of the GRCDA 9th International Landfill Gas Symposium, Newport Beach, 17-21 March 1986.

(4) DEPARTMENT OF THE ENVIRONMENT. Landfilling wastes. Wastes Management Paper No 26, HMSO.

Table 1   Summary of gas collection systems - Phase 2

Gas collection trench	Date of installation	Date when gas abstraction commenced
H2 - Layer 3	February 1985	May 1985
H1 - 'Spur' trench in phase 1	February 1985	February 1985
H2 - Drainage trench	March 1985	-
H1 - Layer 4 (long extension)	May 1985	May 1985
H3 - Layer 4	May 1985	August 1985
H4 - Layer 4	May 1985	August 1985
H4 - Two trenches in layer 5	August 1985	August 1985
H5 - Layer 6	October 1985	)
H6 - Layer 6	October 1985	) Not commenced by
H7 - Layer 6	October 1985	) December 1986
H8 - Layer 3A	June 1986	)
H9 - Layer 3A	June 1986	)
H2A - 3m deep retrofit, NE side of site	September 1986	September 1986
H2B - Pipe to vertical well used for probe tubes	September 1986	September 1986
H2C - Connected to eastern end of H4 layer 4	September 1986	September 1986

Table 2 Advantages and disadvantages of each system

	Advantages	Disadvantages
VERTICAL WELLS	May be installed in the completed part of a site, filled by progressive restoration, while waste is still being deposited in other areas.	Can only be installed in parts of sites which have been brought up to final level therefore some gas may be lost prior to their installation.
	Each well can extract gas from several layers in a deep site.	Specialist drilling contractors are required for installing the wells.
	If the perforated sections extend high enough, a rising leachate level may only partially block the wells and they will still be effective.	If the perforated sections do become blocked by leachate the wells will cease to function. This is more likely to occur in shallow sites where the wells only have short sections of perforations in the base of the site.
HORIZONTAL TRENCHES	Installation of horizontal trenches can be relatively inexpensive because local construction companies may be hired to excavate the trenches.	A deep site may require several layers of trenches and hence become expensive in terms of length of pipe/installation costs.
	Can be readily used for extracting gas from shallow sites.	Only short lengths of trench could be installed at any one time in sites which are being filled in cells or small areas (as per recommended practice).
	May be placed in the higher, unsaturated layers within partially flooded sites.	Trenches in lower levels of waste may become completely blocked by rising leachate and necessitate the installation of more trenches at higher levels.
	May be used to extract gas from lower levels of waste while waste is still being deposited at higher levels.	Uneven settlement in deep sites may result in damage to horizontal pipes.

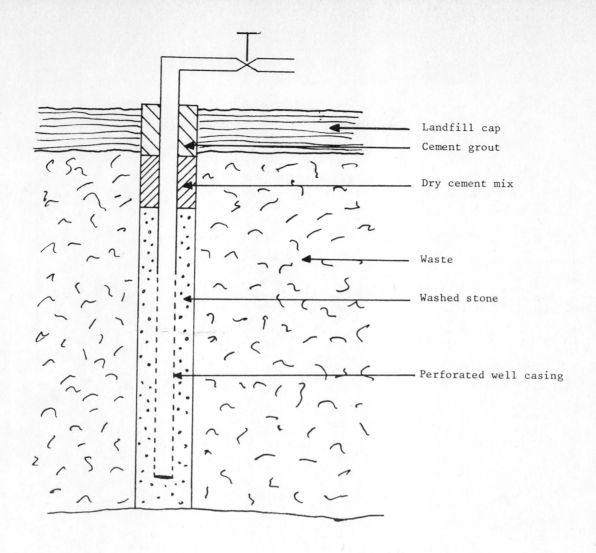

Landfill cap

Cement grout

Dry cement mix

Waste

Washed stone

Perforated well casing

Fig 1   Typical design of vertical well for landfill gas abstraction

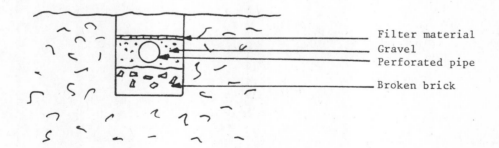

Filter material
Gravel
Perforated pipe

Broken brick

Fig 2   Cross-section of horizontal gas collection trench

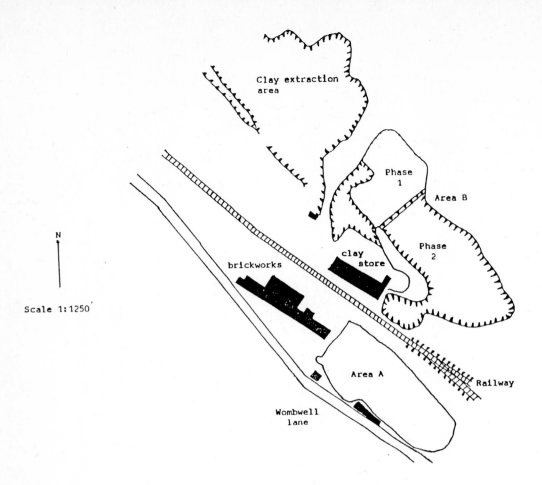

Fig 3   Stairfoot quarries

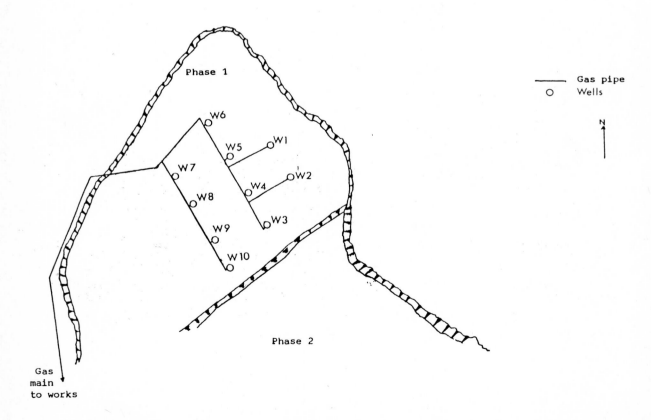

Fig 4   Area B, phase 1 — location of vertical gas extraction wells

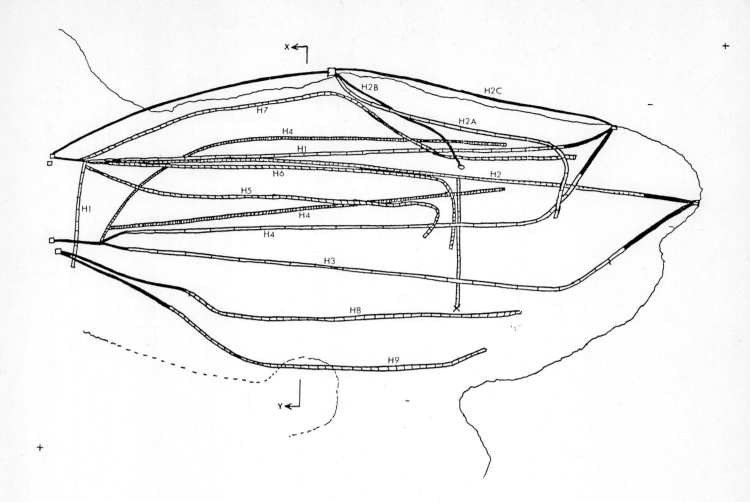

Fig 5   Area B, phase 2 — location of all horizontal trenches

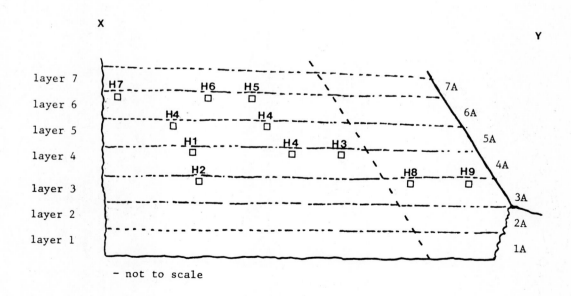

Fig 6   Cross-section of phase 2 showing location of gas collection trenches

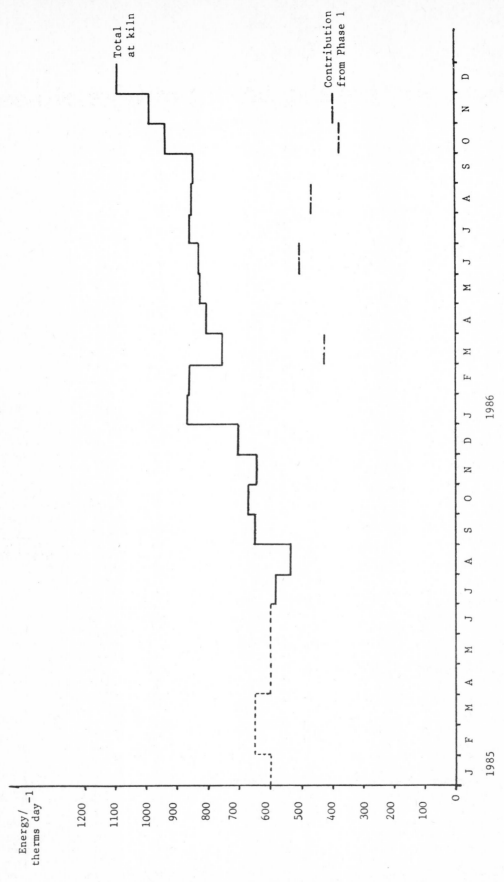

Fig 7   Energy value of landfill gas supplied to the kiln — daily totals
averaged over each month

Landfill gas abstraction and commercial use

H D T MOSS, TD, MA, CEng, MIMechE, MIEE, MInstE
Shanks and McEwan (Southern) Limited, Bedford

<u>SYNOPSIS</u> The duty of care must be recognised by the landfill operator which includes the need to control landfill gas. The gas must be abstracted from the site to ensure that there is no environmental impact through migration or through smell. Suitable methods are discussed. Only when this potential hazard has been harnessed fully, can this valuable energy source be used commercially. The options available are reviewed as well as means of cleaning up the gas to make it more widely usable.

1 INTRODUCTION

Shanks & McEwan (Southern) Limited have been active in landfill gas abstraction for a number of years. The company operates five landfill sites of which three have operational gas abstraction plant, a further two have gas wells already in place with plant currently under construction.

In 1978 the company joined with the Department of Energy and became the first UK organisation to explore the manner in which landfill gas is generated. Harwell Laboratory acted as consultants and subcontractors in a project at the Stewartby landfill site in Bedfordshire which developed into the first scheme to utilise landfill gas commercially. Considerable data was accumulated by the time the project finished in 1982.

Shanks & McEwan (Southern) Limited was formed in 1970 as London Brick Land Development, a part of London Brick Company. In 1977 the name was changed to London Brick Landfill and the company grew in size and sphere of operations. In 1986 London Brick Landfill merged with the Shanks & McEwan Group. With several large refuse disposal contracts, the renamed company continues to have a deep involvement with landfill gas.

By the end of 1987 there will be some eighteen commercial landfill gas recovery and utilisation schemes in the UK. Their combined energy savings, through use of gas both in kilns, furnaces and boilers and in the generation of electricity will amount to over 100 000 tonnes of coal equivalent per annum. Such a level of savings represents a large stride in the use of landfill gas for energy replacement taking the application from development to commercial stature.

2 THE RESOURCE

A total of some 28 million tonnes of domestic, commercial and industrial organic solid waste is generated each year in the United Kingdom.

The domestic waste figure for England and Wales is 13 million tonnes/year. Between 85% and 90% of this is disposed of by landfill whilst the majority of the remainder is disposed of by incineration, most of which is without heat recovery. Much of the balance is used for refuse derived fuel (RDF).

Since 1974, all refuse collection has become the responsibility of District Councils, and in Scotland and Wales they dispose of the refuse also. In England, up to 1986 the disposal was in the hands of the County Councils and Metropolitan County Councils. In England therefore, strategic refuse disposal has become possible. Currently some 10 million tonnes/year domestic refuse are disposed of to sites which contain more than two hundred thousand tonnes. The largest sites will tend to be those serving large areas of population whether by direct disposal or via transfer stations.

There is a tremendous variation in gas yield between the various sites. It makes prediction of site potential difficult unless a gas assay — or proving trial — is undertaken. In such a test, the gas volumes extracted over varying rates are compared with the area of influence shown and extrapolation to take in the whole site gives a reasonable estimate of the potential. However similar sizes of site in similar strata, taking the same categories of waste do show reasonable correlation. Several sources of gas yield for various conditions are available (1, 2 & 3). Overall theoretical gas yield is quoted as being as high as $450m^3$/tonne down to $200m^3$/tonne for average domestic refuse. Practical examples have shown wet active sites producing as much as $22m^3$/tonne/year whereas relatively inactive sites may show only $3m^3$/tonne/year. It is thought that the refuse currently in the larger sites mentioned above, has a potential gas generation rate equivalent to 1.3 million tonnes of coal per annum (4).

3 ABSTRACTION

<u>Wells</u> In the United Kingdom, gas abstraction points are usually called 'wells'. This applies both to the vertically bored holes, as well as to the horizontal trenches. Some wells consist of a series of perforated concrete rings built into the refuse and extended upwards, as the refuse level rises. Others are holes drilled vertically into the refuse from the surface of the completed site. In this case, slotted tubular casing is inserted, the annulus filled with a granular material such as pea gravel and the surface sealed. In other cases, perforated pipes are laid horizontally in trenches in refuse and surrounded by granular material. More refuse is placed on top of the network and yield an efficient means of gathering the landfill gas. Hybrid designs of wells have also been tried but have not yet proved popular (5).

<u>Pipelines:</u> In the work started at Stewartby, the initial vertical wells were connected with PVC pipework which was erected to correct falls by stringing from a series of posts hammered into the landfill surface (6). These networks gave early indications of the way differential settlement affected pipework and also allowed re-stringing when necessary. Subsequent work has used H.D.P.E. pipework below ground. The influence of condensation is substantial, especially in 'wet' sites so burying the pipework whilst maintaining adequate slopes is a preferred method. On large sites gas collection network optimisation is important to ensure the system is cost effective. Furthermore, the depth at which the pipes are placed as well as the falls to which they are laid must also be considered in conjunction with site settlement projections. Due account must be taken of the large amount of liquid removal necessary and the position of such equipment.

<u>Pressure Generators:</u> The first commercial installation in the United Kingdom (Stewartby), used a liquid ring pump. Historically, this equipment had been used successfully for gas movement both in sewage works and in coal mines, two very different yet methane bearing products. Other early schemes followed this lead, partly as the pump acted as a good pressure generator and partly because there was little need to filter water droplets and debris from the gas stream. Other forms of equipment are used such as Rootes-type blowers which are positive displacement machines, cheaper to run than the liquid ring pump and satisfactory with relatively dry gases. Both machines have their advantages and similarly their disadvantages but neither is ideal. Some operators have tried moving vane compressors whilst others are able to achieve sufficient pressure by using high pressure fans. A schematic of the first Stewartby gas compound is shown below as Figure 1.

<u>Flares:</u> A number of types of gas flaring equipment are available for the task of burning off surplus gas or testing new installations. The most popular type uses a travelling flame front to ignite a pilot burner which sustains the main flare.

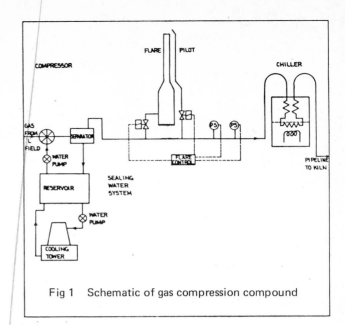

Fig 1   Schematic of gas compression compound

Another type uses a high energy ignition source, usually in constant operation, to sustain ignition. Methane in carbon dioxide requires a relatively large quantity of energy to ignite it, so the choice tends to be between an intermittent propane source (which is easily ignited) and a high energy spark which is a constant consumer of power.

Many landfill gas flares are elevated stacks, as used by refineries. There are cases where County Planning Departments have been unwilling to sanction equipment with such a high impact on the environment. Consequently ground flares also are used, some being refractory lined casings and others 'burn-pits' with fences. In these cases the flames are hidden from sight at the expense of the use of a larger area of ground.

<u>Instrumentation:</u> Where flammable gases are processed, good control must be exercised. With landfill gas there are two constraints, the former arising from the possibility of producing an explosive mixture and the latter from flame instability caused by low calorific value. Already a standard has evolved in the industry whereby an oxygen meter is obligatory for any commercial installation (7). With the larger schemes, methane monitoring is considered important as well. The philosophy of the scheme needs to be matched with the degree of control and extent of information required. Whilst there is a trend towards data logging of information, it is also necessary to satisfy the potential customer that they will be receiving the energy quantities stated. In this respect flow meters and calorimeters should be used as back-up evidence.

<u>Moisture Removal:</u> Mention has already been made of the potential problems caused by condensation. Moisture knock out is essential, and depending on the gas flows and the machinery used, pre-filters may also be necessary. In generating pressure, work is done on the gas such that it usually leaves the machinery above the new dew point. In applications where the gas is flared or is

consumed close to the plant, there may be no need for further moisture removal. Where a pipeline of some length is required, some extra form of moisture removal becomes essential. Many applications use a stainless steel version of a compressed air drier, using refrigeration to cool the gases to 275°K. Some plants reheat the outgoing gas with the incoming moisture laden gas and achieve a low relative humidity gas.

4 COMMERCIAL OPTIONS

The landfill operator has a duty to protect the environment, one aspect of which is the need to control landfill gases. In the process of doing so, these measures must not create a different form of pollution. The gas collected must be burned safely by using a properly designed flaring system. Commercialisation can only be considered if the site operated is adequately controlled and continuous and regularly monitored abstraction exercised. However, once this state has been reached, commercialism is a "bolt-on" extra. The apparent differences in costings for plant arise mainly from the different accounting philosophies. The first Stewartby compound is run as an environmental unit whose byproduct is used for burning bricks. If taken as an overall commercial scheme it would not make a trading surplus.

Many landfill sites are located away from centres of population which makes the choice of a suitable end user, rather more difficult. Where there is a choice it is preferable to be able to supply energy to a consumer with a constant load, using a high value source of primary fuel. An ideal customer would have a process load typically running at an average of 70% to 80% of the maximum demand and using (say) bulk propane. A rather less suitable target would be a consumer using large quantities of energy mainly in the winter months and burning low grade coal. The type of load varies with the industry but Table 1 illustrates typical prices charged for common fuels.

Table 1

Typical prices of readily available energy

Industrial electricity	110p/therm		10.4£/GJ		
Domestic electricity	150p	"	14.2	"	
Gas oil	40p	"	3.6	"	
Propane	44p	"	4.2	"	
Domestic natural gas	37p	"	3.5	"	
Bulk supply natural gas	33p	"	3.1	"	
Coal	24p	"	2.3	"	

Where no substantial direct gas users are available close to a landfill site, electricity generation may prove an attractive option. Both engines or turbines can be modified to run on landfill gas and the energy harnessed to produce electricity. Germany and the USA have several examples of the use of landfill gas in both types of machine. Most of these have been very successful but in a few cases trace quantities of thiols and halocarbons have caused severe corrosion. In most cases this has started with a breakdown

of the engine oil through acidification. Many schemes have considerable operating experience and base their monitoring on the quality of the engine oil at regular intervals and frequent engine oil changes. It is prudent to assess the trace constituents of the gases in the design stage of a scheme. The list of possible constituents is extensive (7) but the concentrations vary according to the type of waste and its age.

So far few UK plants use any substantial form of gas clean-up. Most of the larger ones condense out the majority of the moisture before putting the gas in a pipeline but only two of the electricity generation schemes contemplate gas scrubbing before use. A list of all the plants appears as Table 2 (4).

5 GAS TREATMENT

Water washing of the pressurised gas is the simplest form of removing both trace contaminants and the majority of the carbon dioxide. Three sewerage works in the UK produce biogas from the anaerobic digestion of their sludge. This gas is very similar to landfill gas and with pressurised water clean-up can yield 98% pure methane. When compressed to 200 bar (3,000 psig) and stored in cylinders it can be used as a vehicle fuel.

These water authorities run vehicles on the compressed gas instead of on petrol and, with diesel-engined vehicles, substitute part of the diesel by gas.

However many landfill sites where gas clean-up is an economic option produce much larger volumes of gas than sewerage works. In consequence larger quantities of water would be required to produce the nearly pure methane and the resulting contaminated effluent would itself require considerable treatment. In addition the appreciable solubility of methane, whilst still less than that of carbon dioxide would mean that significant quantities would be lost during water scrubbing. The result is that other forms of separation are used such as membranes, absorption by liquids and adsorption by solids.

Membrane separation: This is based on the principle that certain gas species pass through a membrane faster than other species. This permeation is a combination of solution into the membrane and diffusion through the membrane. The efficiency varies according to the wall thickness and material properties of the membrane. Typically carbon dioxide is the 'fast gas' which permeates through the membrane leaving a methane rich stream.

In the Mansanto Prism[R] process, the raw landfill gas is compressed to between 17 bar and 53 bar (250 and 800 psig). The gas passes down bundles of hollow fibre membranes within a metal shell. Typically the product contains 75% to 80% methane so further units must be used to allow further purification.

In the Separex[TM] process, the membranes are spirally wound round a central perforated core. Permeation rates are faster than those for the Prism[R] system so lower pressures can

Table 2 — UK Landfill Gas Exploitation Schemes — From Ref 4

Gas Produced	Use	Start Date	*TCEPA Savings as at Dec 87
Shanks &McEwan, Stewartby	Brick Kilns	1981	5600
Normanton Brick	Kilns	1981	800
Campbell Brick	Kilns	1982	2160
Yorkshire Brick	Kilns	1983	1200+
Aveley Methane	Water Tube Boiler X	1983	20000
Bidston Methane	Shell Boiler	1985	6200
Land Fill Gas Ltd	Shell Boiler	1985	1300
Lemace	Shell Boiler (Horticulture)	1985	80
Blue Circle	Kilns	1985	35000
Wimpey Waste/Mainsprint	Boilers	1985	1600
Merseyside Waste	Electricity – gas engines	1985	4150
ARC	Electricity – gas engines	1986	2075
Cleanaway	Leachate treatment	1986	(small)
Maltby Brick	Kilns	1986/7	2500
Shanks & McEwan, Arlesey	Brick Drier	1987	1060
Shanks & McEwan, Stewartby	Electricity – gas engines	1987	3320
Peel	Electricity – turbine	1987	14525
Greenland Reclamation	Electricity-dual fuel engines	1987	12450

*TCEPA = Tonnes of Coal Equivalent per annum   X With Gas Turbine from 1987

be used. However the smaller surface areas available to gas contact mean that larger units are required for similar volumes of gas.

Liquid absorption: Several plants have been built which clean up landfill gas using the physical and chemical absorption by liquids. The Selexol Process uses glycols as a solvent to remove carbon dioxide, hydrogen sulphide and water. The solvent can be recovered easily and the absorbed gas released at low pressure. Material loss and regeneration costs are low.

The Kryosol Process uses methanol under pressure at -35°C and -75°C. The first step removes halocarbons and heavy hydrocarbons and the next step removes the carbon dioxide. Several stages of flashing are required to separate the carbon dioxide. A third process uses monoethanolamine (MEA) or diethanolamine (DEA). Landfill gas at pressures around 20 bar to 25 bar (300 psig to 375 psig) is fed into towers where counter current contact leaves pipeline quality methane. The absorbent is reclaimed by a series of flashings or by steam stripping but some of this is degraded by the carbon dioxide. MEA degrades more readily than DEA but the DEA is more difficult to reclaim.

Solid adsorption: Molecular sieves are the most commonly used absorbents of carbon dioxide from landfill gas. These are a range of calcium alumino silicates packed in towers. They are very sensitive to contamination and often are preceded by silica gel or glycol towers to remove water and by activated carbon to remove the higher molecular weight contaminants. Various methods of pressure and temperature variation are used to regenerate the materials with the result that the plants are relatively energy intensive.

REFERENCES

(1) 'State of the art Methane Gas Enhancement in Landfills'.
     Angonne Nat. Lab., June 1981.
     DOE W–31–109–ENG38.

(2) Rees, J. F.
     'The face of carbon compounds in the landfill disposal of organic matter'.
     J. Chem. Tech. Biotechnol 30 (1980) p162.

(3) Stegmann, R.
     'Grundlagen der Deponieentgasung – Basisinformationen uber die Enstehung von Deponiegas'.
     Europaisches Deponiegas Forum. Munich 1986.

(4) Richards, K. M.
     'Landfill Gas – The sweet smell of success'.
     5th International Conference – Energy Options in the World Scene. University of Reading, April 1987.

(5) Moss, H. D. T, Manley, B. J. W.
     'Review of Landfill Gas Field Projects'
     Shanks & McEwan (Southern) Limited.
     Energy from Landfill Gas Conference, Solihull, October 1986.

(6) Cheyney, A. C, Moss, H. D. T.
     'Landfill Gas as an Energy Source'.
     Landfill Gas Symposium, Harwell, May 1981.

(7) Department of Environment, Waste Management Paper No. 26. ISBN 0 11 7518913.

Landfill gas—the potential for profit

C A R BIDDLE, LLB, FRSA
Packington Estate Enterprises Limited, Meriden, Coventry
E NAYLOR, CEng, FICE, FIMechE, FIEE and **A STREET**, BSC(Eng),MICE, MIWEM
MRM Partnership, Clifton, Bristol

SYNOPSIS   A number of operational schemes have been developed in the UK where landfill gas is either being used directly as a fuel or for generating electricity. One of the largest such projects is being developed at the Packington Lane Landfill Site, situated midway between Birmingham and Coventry.

1   INTRODUCTION

During the last ten years or so there has been a rapid growth in the number of operational and proposed landfill gas recovery and utilisation schemes. Indeed, landfill gas is rapidly becoming an accepted fuel in the brick, cement and related quarrying-based industries.

Refuse disposal sites produce substantial quantities of methane and other gases during their anaerobic decomposition phase. The processes by which landfill gas is produced and the properties of the gas itself have been widely reported elsewhere (1, 2, 3). Briefly, landfill gas is produced as a result of bacterial decay of the waste materials lying within the landfill. The gas typically contains 50 to 60 per cent methane, with the balance being made up of Carbon Dioxide, relatively small percentages of Nitrogen and Oxygen, and a wide variety of trace compounds. Landfill-derived gas has a calorific value about half that of natural gas.

The quantity of gas recovered from one tonne of refuse can vary considerably, being largely dependent upon site specific operational and gas collection techniques. The importance of developing gas recovery and utilisation schemes as an integral part of the original planning, design, operation and restoration proposals for the landfill sites involved has been highlighted by Campbell (4).

It is recognised that there are three major uses for landfill gas (5, 6), i.e.

(a)   Direct use in kilns, furnaces and boilers: This is the simplest and most straight-forward use, although somewhat dependent on there being a direct user for the gas reasonably close to the landfill.

(b)   Full treatment of gas to upgrade to a higher calorific value fuel: This can be a very expensive operation and has not been undertaken commercially to date in the UK, although there are operational schemes in the USA.

(c)   Electricity generation using gas engines or turbines: Landfill gas is an acceptable fuel for reciprocating gas engines or gas turbines, and since the introduction of the 1983 Energy Act, Local Area Electricity Boards are compelled to purchase power produced by private generators at a published tariff, subject only to technical objections. A dual arrangement is also possible where the electricity generated may be used internally, with the surplus power fed into the local grid.

A number of operational schemes have been developed in the UK where landfill gas is either being used directly as fuel or for generating electricity. One of the largest such projects is being developed by Packington Environmental Energy Resources Ltd., a wholly owned subsidiary of Packington Estate Enterprises Ltd. (PEEL) who operate a 155 hectare controlled landfill between Birmingham and Coventry (Figure 1).

2   THE PACKINGTON LANDFILL GAS PROJECT

The landfill site is part of the 2000 hectare Packington Estate owned by the Earl of Aylesford, his son, the Lord Guernsey, and various family trusts. Their Lordships hold seats on the Board of PEEL and take an active part in the operation of the Company.

The site receives in excess of 600 000 tonnes of waste per annum, comprising domestic, commercial and industrial wastes, with a relatively high proportion of Special Wastes. The current planning permission allows tipping up to 50 metres above natural contours, and provides some 18 million cubic metres of void for filling.

The Waste Disposal Site Licence issued by the Warwickshire County Council, in accordance with the Control of Pollution Act 1974, states that the operators of the Packington Estate Enterprises Ltd. Waste Disposal Landfill Site be required to manage the site in a safe and adequate manner (7). Such safe management requires that a means be established to control the potential hazard which exists due to the formation of methane gas within the landfill.

Furthermore, the Royal Commission on Environmental Pollution, in their Eleventh Report, 'Managing Waste: The Duty of Care', Command Paper No. 9675 dated December 1985, endorses the requirements of the Waste Disposal Site Licence. The Commission recommends '....that all licences for new landfill sites should require provision for adequate control of methane, both during and after the period of deposition of wastes...' (8).

At Little Packington, landfill gas is not seen as a problem but as a commercial asset. In fact, PEEL are concerned to optimise gas production to the extent of controlling the type of waste accepted at the site. At Packington, therefore, whilst not ignoring the potential hazards, considerable emphasis is placed on the potential for profit.

A pioneering scheme was initiated at Packington some three years ago, and a technical feasibility study undertaken to appraise engineering proposals to utilise landfill gas from the Little Packington Landfill Site. The study clearly indicated that a landfill gas utilisation scheme offered a technically feasible solution to neutralising the hazardous nature of the gas, whilst offering a significant potential profit, which was shown to more than offset the costs of control otherwise involved.

This approach is clearly in line with the Royal Commission on Environmental Pollution, which, in its Eleventh Report, supports initiatives to utilise the low calorific landfill gas as an energy source and suggests the need for innovative approaches in the utilisation of what is otherwise a hazardous waste fuel.

The Packington Landfill Gas Project is now well advanced, with the generating plant due to be commissioned in October 1987. The project, which will cost in excess of £2 million, is among the first in the UK to utilise a gas turbine to produce electrical power, using landfill gas as the prime fuel. The background to the project is briefly described in the following sections of this paper.

3   QUALITY AND QUANTITY OF LANDFILL GAS

Since 1981 a comprehensive system of landfill gas wells has been installed at Packington (Figure 2). These consist of vertical pipes joining horizontal perforated pipes laid in an artificial geological pipe of pea gravel during the refuse filling process. Areas filled prior to 1981 have been accessed by means of drilled wells and perforated vertical pipes; wells vary in depth from 8 metres to 30 metres. The wells have been interconnected by means of a gas collection main incorporating sampling points and valves. As the landfill gas is saturated, the influence of condensation is considerable; burying the pipework whilst maintaining adequate falls is therefore essential. In designing the gas collection network, careful consideration has been given to future site settlement, site development, and possible temperature effects from the waste decompositon process. Experience on site has shown High Density Polyethylene

(HDPE) to be the most satisfactory material for gas pipelines, being chemically resistant both to the gas and condensate.

Settlement after completion of tipping can pose considerable problems and can have a disastrous effect on the gas collection network. Indeed, at one very deep site in the U.S. a complete 14 inch diameter steel ring main was lost as a result of excessive settlement.

The high densities achieved at Little Packington appear to have provided the best answer yet to settlement problems. The method of tipping at the tip face is perhaps the best controlled in the UK. The working face is constantly kept below a height of 1 metre, with compactors continuously at work to provide a surface suitable for incoming vehicles to drive over, and thereby increase the compaction densities, thus minimising settlement. 'As-laid' densities at Little Packington are amongst the highest recorded in the industry, with regularly measured values exceeding 1.2 tonnes per cubic metre since 1980.

The quality and quantity of gas produced within the landfill has been established by test pumping, the rate of flow from known wells being in excess of 2000 cubic feet per minute (3400 cubic metres per hour), with an average calorific value of around 450 Btu's per cubic foot.

4   CHOICE OF PRIME MOVER

All potential uses for the gas from the Packington Landfill site were evaluated in detail. On the basis of this evaluation, it was considered that the generation of electrical energy for export to the public electricity supply network offered the best solution.

On the basis of the proven quantity and quality of landfill gas produced at Packington, the decision was taken to examine the feasibility of utilising a gas turbine driven alternator, and proposals submitted by Centrax Limited (Gas Turbine Division) were duly evaluated. The use of a gas turbine was, at the time, novel in the UK, and has several simple advantages over the more commonly used reciprocating gas engines. In particular:

(a)   Carbon Dioxide, which comprises up to 40 per cent by volume of landfill gas and is normally a waste product in energy conversion, can be used by the turbine to generate electricity. This is simply because the gas turbine operates by utilising the expansive properties of all gases in the landfill gas mixture; thus, the scheme can come on stream earlier and remain operational longer.

(b)   A very high combustion temperature of 1035 degrees is used, which has the added environmental advantage of destroying the toxic compounds within the landfill gas mixture.

(c)   Guaranteed and lower overhaul costs – indeed, the lowest cost option per installed kilowatt hour.

(d) For many sites the gas turbine is probably too large. However, for a site the size of Packington the turbine comes into its own.

Centrax Ltd. were able to offer a well-proven assembly (more commonly used in powering the Hercules C130 military transport plane), comprising an Allison Turbine single shaft engine utilising a 14-stage axial flow compressor, six combustion chambers within an annular compressor, and a four stage turbine, with a compression ratio of 9:3:1. The engine, when running at speed, is governed to 14000 r/min and geared to drive a four pole, three-phase, 11000 V air-cooled brushless alternator, of BRUSH manufacture, capable of producing 4.5 Mega watts terminal power. After allowing for parasitic losses associated with energy requirements for gas cleaning and compression, some 3.7 Mega watts of electrical energy will be available for export.

5   TURBINE PERFORMANCE

The gas requirements of the turbine are related to the calorific value of the gas at a temperature of 0°C. On the assumpton that the turbine alternator set were to achieve only 95 per cent of the manufacturer's rated efficiency, the gas flow requirements can be calculated, as illustrated by Figure 3. It can be seen that, assuming the average calorific value of the gas can, by selective blending from the wells, be controlled at 450 Btu's per cubic foot, then a flow of 1760 cubic feet per minute from the gas field would produce, at the minimum rated efficiency, an electrical output at the alternator terminals of 4 Mega watts. Centrax have in fact guaranteed that the turbine alternator will operate satisfactorily producing the power output, as set out in their specification, utilising landfill gas with a calorific value which may vary between 375 and 500 Btu's per cubic foot at 0°C. The unit was tested prior to delivery with a gas at 375 Btu's, and gave 105 per cent performance against design rating.

Performance details provided by the turbine manufacturer relating to gas usage were based on natural gas. Whilst landfill gas has a lower calorific value, it also contains some 50 to 55 per cent of non-combustible gas, mainly CO_2 and N_2, which add to the total volume flow of gas through the turbine, resulting in an increase in output of around 3 per cent when compared to the same calorific value of natural gas.

Ambient air temperature affects the turbine output; at lower temperatures air has a greater density, thus producing higher outputs for a given gas input.

6   SYSTEM OPERATION

Suction will be applied to the gas collection system using a high pressure suction fan, with the pressure varied on each well-head to control the quantity and quality of gas extracted (investigations undertaken by PEEL into grid operation in the USA indicate that it is desirable to restrict the rate of flow from a well in order to maintain a constant calorific value over a sustained period of time).

The landfill gas, after extraction, will flow up to 2 kilometres to processing equipment where cleansing takes place using a wet scrubber. The gas will enter the scrubber near the base, passing first through a dense water spray to saturate and cool the gas to its adiabatic saturation temperature. Saturated gases then pass upwards through impingement baffle plates where intensive scrubbing occurs. Intimate gas-liquid contact will remove the soluble gaseous components, and impingement on the wetted baffles will precipitate any solid particles which are then removed in the scrubbing liquid. The scrubber will be operated on a continuously recirculated liquor basis.

From the scrubber the supply of gas will enter the suction side of two three-stage gas compressors. After the final stage of compression, the gas passes through a shell and tube heat exchanger and air blast aftercooler; this method of compression and cooling eliminates 99.9 per cent moisture. Any hydrocarbons (in liquid form) which remain will be gasified by heating and the gas, now at a pressure of 17 BAR, then passes into the turbine. System operation is illustrated schematically by Figure 4.

7   ELECTRICAL POWER PRODUCTION

In order to calculate the operational time for the turbine alternator, it is necessary to evaluate the plant down-time. Centrax Ltd. have advised that service requirements would be as follows:

General monthly service - 1 No. 8 hr shift/month

The General Service will be incorporated within the following extended services:

    4000 hr service (6 monthly)   96 hrs down-time
    8000 hr service (12 monthly)   288 hrs down-time
   16000 hr service (24 monthly)   432 hrs down-time
   32000 hr service (36 monthly) 1008 hrs down-time

The resultant pattern of servicing, over a period of 12¼ years, is illustrated by Figure 5.

Calculations for the production of electrical power have been based on an 8760 hour year (1986), in which the down-time is that shown for Year 1 in Figure 5, i.e. 464 hours. The productive hours for such a year are therefore 8760 less 464 hours, i.e. 8296 hours; this is termed the 'NORMAL YEAR'. Calculations for electrical power production for the normal year are summarised by Figure 6.

In order to calculate the revenue from the sale of electrical power for the normal year, tariff information was derived from information published by the Midlands Electricity Board. Following discussions with the PEEL Management, it was agreed that routine maintenance would be undertaken at times when the 'sale price' of electrical power was at its lowest (the period

23.30 to 07.30 hours has therefore been selected to meet this criterion for the general monthly eight-hour duration service).

A value for the sale of electrical power for each month has been derived from calculations to determine the value of 1 kilowatt output during each month, multiplied by the average saleable kilowatt output for that month (as shown in Figure 4). Allowing for adjustments for the Fuel Charge, the Capacity Charge and Standing Charge, in accordance with the Midlands Electricity Board Tariff, the annual nett income from the sale of electrical power is calculated to be around £740 000. This, of course, is not pure profit.

8   COSTS

In assessing the costs, it must be remembered that in the absence of a scheme to utilise the gas there would be considerable cost merely in controlling the hazard (ref. Royal Commission on Environmental Pollution, 11th Report). Therefore, costs for generation, which would otherwise be considered to be excessive, have been accepted, thus leading to a further reduction in return on capital. The lack of return is further exacerbated by the reductions already announced in tariffs, and, indeed, future reductions cannot be ruled out.

The effect of service down-time on potential revenue has not been ignored. Indeed, during extended services a replacement turbine will be hired in order to minimise the loss in revenue. A discounted cash flow analysis for the project over a period of 11¼ years has shown that the cost of providing a replacement unit during extended service periods (in excess of 96 days) is far outweighed by the income from sale of electrical power generated using the replacement unit.

At the time of writing the paper, commissioning had only just been completed and no figures can therefore be quoted, either for revenue or costs.

9   CONCLUDING REMARKS

It is recognised that, in many instances, bio-fuels, of which landfill gas is one, represent a very valuable source of energy. At Packington this potential is being realised, with the land-fill effectively being used as a power station generating enough electricity to cover the needs of about 5000 homes or a town the size of Warwick. Packington Envirionmental Energy Resources Ltd. are, therefore avoiding losses in controlling what would otherwise be a hazard. This, indeed, is engineering for profit from waste.

The Packington Landfill Gas Project has caught the imagination of many, including the Government. In closing, a quotation from the Keynote Address given by Mr. David Hunt, MBE, MP, Parliamentary Under Secretary of State for Energy, at the Energy From Landfill Gas Conference held in October 1986 in Solihull, seems particularly relevant:

'...I would like to say a few words about Packington Estate Enterprises Ltd. because it is our most recent and, I think, most ambitious and exciting landfill gas demonstration project. Packington Estate Enterprises ... has, with the help of my Department's Energy Efficiency Office, embarked on a two million pound project to generate three and a half Mega watts of electricity from landfill gas and export it to the national grid. I wholeheartedly commend this initiative...' (9)

10   ACKNOWLEDGEMENTS

The authors acknowledge permission given by PEEL and MRM Partnership for the publication of this paper.

REFERENCES

(1)   DEPARTMENT OF THE ENVIRONMENT, Waste Management Paper No. 26 Landfilling Wastes, 1986.

(2)   Proceedings of ENERGY FROM LANDFILL GAS Conference, 28-31 August 1986.

(3)   Proceedings of LANDFILL GAS SYMPOSIUM, 6 May 1981 (Harwell).

(4)   CAMPBELL, D.J.V.   Landfill Management Techniques in Relation to Landfill Gas Abstraction and Utilization, Proceedings of Energy from Landfill Gas Conference, 1986, 22-31.

(5)   RICHARDS, K.M., Progress of Landfill Gas as a Fuel, March 1986.

(6)   COUNTY SURVEYORS SOCIETY, Report Number 4/4, Coping with Landfill Gas, May 1987.

(7)   Waste Disposal Site Licence for the Packington Lane Landfill Site, issued by Warwickshire County Council.

(8)   ROYAL COMMISSION ON ENVIRONMENTAL POLLUTION, Eleventh Report, Managing Waste : The Duty of Care, Command Paper 9675, December 1985.

(9)   HUNT, D.   Keynote Address, Energy from Landfill Gas Conference 28-31 August 1986.

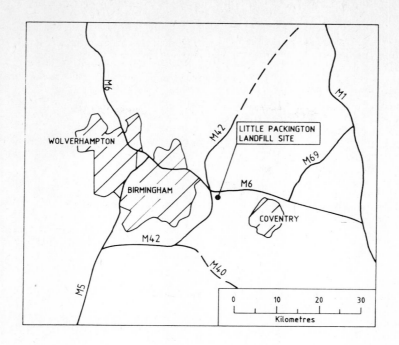

Fig 1   Location of the Little Packington landfill site

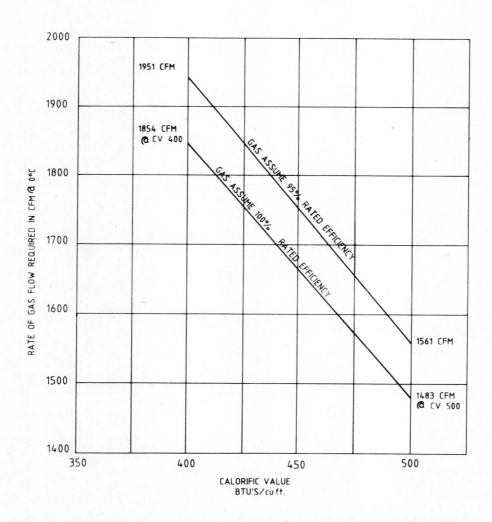

Fig 3   Gas flow required to achieve minimal 4 MVA at alternator terminals

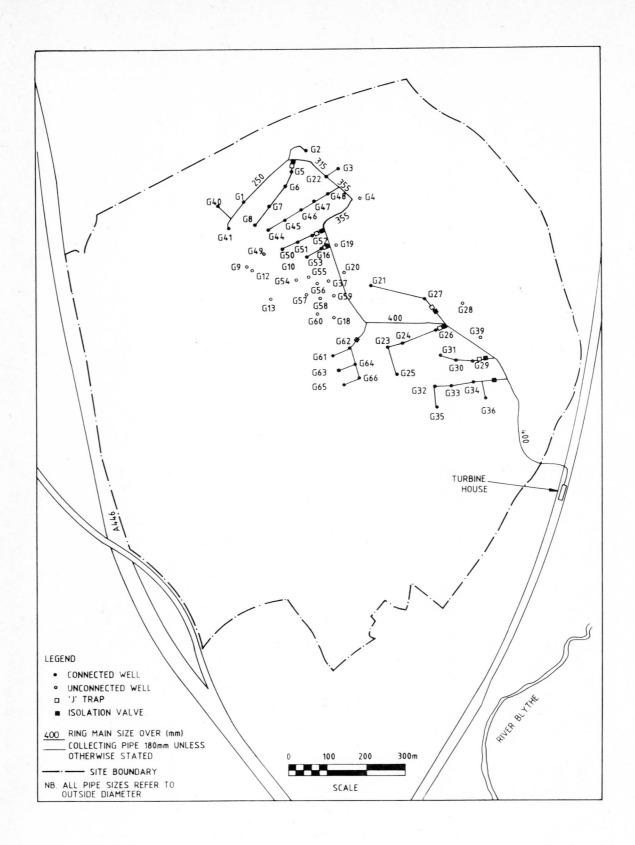

Fig 2   Gas well network

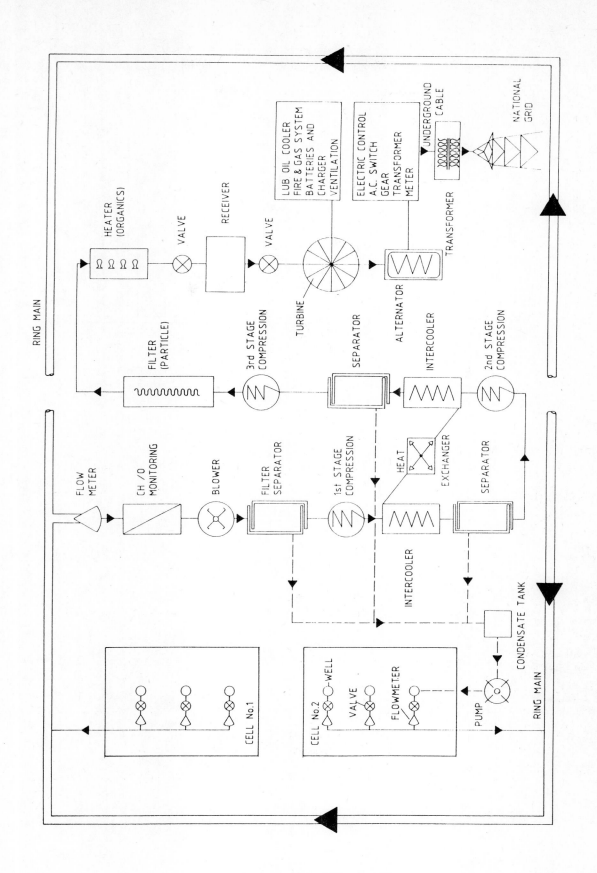

Fig 4   Schematic of system operation

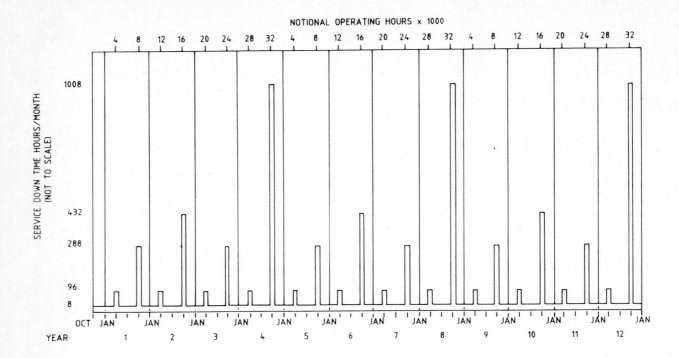

Fig 5   Service down-time

ELECTRICAL POWER PRODUCTION

	JAN	FEB	MAR	APR	MAY	JUNE	JULY	AUG	SEPT	OCT	NOV	DEC
Average ambient monthly temperature B. Amper	3.70	3.37	5.47	7.42	10.43	14.19	16.52	16.19	13.46	10.02	6.85	4.20
Average monthly kW output @ 100%	3950	3950	3900	3840	3750	3670	3600	3620	3680	3750	3860	3920
Assume increase of 3% due to landfill gas	4069	4069	4017	3955	3863	3780	3708	3729	3790	3863	3976	4038
Assume m/c 95%	3866	3866	3816	3757	3670	3591	3523	3543	3601	3670	3777	3836
Deduct 450 kW for auxiliaries to give saleable power kW	3416	3416	3366	3307	3220	3141	3073	3093	3151	3220	3327	3386
Operating hours/	736	664	736	624	736	712	736	736	712	456	712	736
Saleable KWH	2514 176	2268 224	2477 376	2063 568	2369 920	2236 392	2261 728	2276 448	2243 512	1468 320	2368 824	2492 096

TOTAL 27040 584

Fig 6   Electrical power production for the 'normal year'

C09/88

Landfill methane gas utilization—electricity power generation

E MATAN, MSc, CEng, FIMechE, FIMarE, MICE, FBIM
Matan and Partners Limited, Liverpool
A F POTTER, BSc, FICE
Merseyside Development Corporation, Liverpool

SYNOPSIS In 1984, Britain's first International Garden Festival was established on a previously derelict landfill site in Liverpool. There were considerable amounts of landfill gas that, if uncollected, would have killed every tree on the site and created envrironmental hazards. This paper describes the gas collection system and the pioneering work carried out to utilise the landfill gas for electricity power generation.

1   INTRODUCTION

The design, construction and organisation of the International Garden Festival on 125 acres of former rubbish tip, oil tank installations and degraded shoreline, following one of the largest reclamation schemes ever undertaken in Western Europe was completed on time at the end of April 1984.

On 2nd May 1984 the International Garden Festival was opened by Her Majesty the Queen, accompanied by HRH the Duke of Edinburgh. Her Majesty spoke of the relevance of organising a Garden Festival in a derelict area of Liverpool and emphasised that the gardens and exhibitions blooming on this site are symbolic of what we all wish for Liverpool.

When the Festival closed in September, three and a half million people had visited the gardens. Beneath the feet of those visitors, 10 million tons of domestic refuse was generating the gas that, uncollected, would have killed every tree on the site and driven the visitors reeling from the smell.

Otterspool, which forms part of the International Garden Festival site, is located some 7km south of the Pier Head, Liverpool, by the River Mersey. The Otterspool site consists of 40.5 hectares of reclaimed land, created by the construction of a sea wall from the Dingle to Otterspool promenade. The area behind the sea wall, upto the original shore/cliff line, was filled between 1957 and 1981 with about 6 million cubic metres of predominantly domestic refuse to a normal depth of 10 metres. The site was originally established by Liverpool City Council and was taken over by the Merseyside Development Corporation and it was developed for use as the International Garden Festival.

The formidable task of transforming the waste disposal site, together with other derelict land, rubbish tip, tank farms and degraded shoreline within the Riverside area, into the now famous and successful Britain's first International Garden Festival is well appreciated and regarded by millions of people as remarkable. The technical achievement, most of which is invisible, is even more remarkable. From the initial site investigation, it was apparent that there was a considerable amount of landfill gas generated at the site. The methane gas extraction system was installed at a cost of just under £1 million and the gas was being flared to waste since 1983.

2   METHANE GAS EXTRACTION SYSTEM

Two main types of systems were tried at pilot scale. The fist and cheapest used the principle that the gas rising to the surface takes the most porous path. An inverted drainage system of stone filled trenches collected and led the gas to high points of the site. This system had only very localised effects and produced explosive mixtures in the trench. The second system that proved totally effective used pumped boreholes. The boreholes perforated above the water table to within 5m of the ground level had an effective collection radius of upto 70m. The system required a nominal clay seal to keep air from the surface out. The collection system is in two parts. The northern half consists of 26 boreholes within the Festival Gardens site, 3 boreholes just outside the Festival Gardens south boundary fence and a borehole by the Methane Gas Compressor Section. These are connected to the Methane Gas Compressor Station.

The southern half which forms the south shore site consists of 7 boreholes. The site is connected to the station, but can be isolated by closing the main isolation valve to the site. Gas is drawn from both parts of the Otterspool Site to the Methane Gas Compressor Station.

The Methane Gas Compressor Station is situated outside the Festival Gardens Site, to the south by the promenade. The Station was completed in December 1983 and testing of plant and equipment commenced in January 1984 with final commissioning in March 1984. Gas entering the station passes through knock out pots and filters to two gas compressors which are arranged as duty/standby. The Compressors are CompAir, Broomwade VML1000 twin dry cylinder, vee-belt driven, reciprocating gas compressors. Each compressor is capable of 1656 cub.m/hr at an inlet suction of 87 mbar and discharge pressure of 1.3 bar which was the initial design condition for flaring or 1500 c.m/hr similar suction and 2.7 bar discharge pressure for the gas engines. From the duty gas compressor, the gas passes through an after-cooler to the inlets of the gas engine plant. If the gas engines are not in operation the gas can be passed to the flare stack for flaring. The total cost of the methane gas extraction system is just under £1 million.

3 METHANE GAS UTILISATION OPTIONS

The main priority for the Otterspool landfill site was to make the site safe, not just for the immediate use of the International Garden Festival, but for the long term use of the land and safety of the surrounding area. The ground monitor results, kept by Messrs. Matan and Partners, demonstrate the success of the methane gas extraction system and its effectiveness in reducing the methane in the top-soil and sub-soil layers to a negligible level. There is no evidence of die-back of growth due to gas and all odour nuisances have been eliminated. The success story of the International Garden Festival would not have been possible without the successful methane gas extraction at the site. In order to maintain the safety of the site and the surrounding area, it will be necessary to continue the operation of the gas extraction system for the next 15 to 20 years.

The priority stated above and the environmental considerations are desirable and certainly essential for the establishment of the Festival Gardens and to resolve the undesirable and hazardous situations. The methane content of the gas, however, constitutes a valuable energy source. It certainly does not make economic sense to continue flaring the gas to waste. The value of the available energy being burnt away, the operating cost of the plant, not to mention the initial capital expenditure involved in recovering the gas, makes it imperative to find a viable use for the gas.

Considerable effort has been expended in the quest for commercial utilisation of the methane gas and many schemes have been considered and rejected on economic grounds. These included direct sale of the gas to local industrial customers. Other options examined included the conversion of the gas to liquified natural gas, conversion to methanol (methyl alcohol), direct combustion for space heating locally and the option for the gas to be used for electricity power generation.

The utilisation of the methane gas for electricity power generation was found to be a commercially viable proposition. In addition to the electricity power generated, the recoverable heat from the waste heat provides a potential source of energy. The investment appraisal carried out on the Methane Gas Utilisation Scheme was very lengthy and this was carried out in stages, initially to satisfy the safety and environmental consideration of the Festival Garden site. This was followed by a detailed technical and economic evaluation for commercial exploitation of the gas. Risk and uncertainty played a very important role in the economic appraisal of the methane gas utilisation. The risk of explosion was apparent, but the uncertainty surrounding the technology required was rather more worrying. A thorough technical evaluation was therefore carried out followed by an economic evaluation. At all stages of the evaluation, allowances had to made made for the uncertainty involved - uncertainty surrounding the gas yield from the boreholes, bio-chemical reactions, performance of the gas extraction system etc. The figures for financial appraisal have been arrived at after considering the most pessimistic outcome in every case, from gas production levels to volume of gas availability in subsequent years and the resultant income from the sale of electricity generated. The financial appraisal was based on a project life of 12 years and was based on financial viablity only. It does not take into account any "economic" environmental benefits which may occur, such as reduced odour nuisance, vegetation die-back or gas migration control. The estimated payback period for the generation scheme is 4 years.

4 GAS CHARACTERISTICS/AVAILABILITY

Landfill gas is very variable in composition. Its variablity depends upon the characteristics of the refuse and the ways in which it has been put into the landfill (tipping, composting and covering etc) and the ways in which the gas is taken off. The ranges of constituents of landfill gas are: Methane 45-65 percent V/V, Carbon Dioxide 34-45 percent V/V, Hydrogen 0-1 percent, Nitrogen 0-1 percent, Oxygen 0-1 percent, Hydrogen Sulphide 0-100ppm, Ammonia trace, other organics 5ppm.

The calorific value is in the range of 16–23 MJ/cubic metres compared with natural gas of 38.5 MJ/cubic metres. Methane gas is lighter than air, with specific gravity of about 0.5 (air–1).

At the Otterspool Site, the site was continually over pumped with the methane content of the gas as low as 22–28 percent most of the time during the period of the International Garden Festival in 1984. The total gas production is conservatively estimated at 53 TJ/annum, about 6MW. The estimated gas availability is given in the summary of technical details.

5 ELECTRICITY POWER GENERATION PLANT

The Power Generation Plant has been installed at a cost of £525.000. Site testing and commissioning took place in May 1986 and power generation commenced early in June 1986.

The Methane Gas Power Generation Scheme consists of two Caterpillar G399, turbo-charged, after-cooled engines, driving Caterpillar SR4 brushless alternators, capable of generating 1MW of electricity at 415 volts and a Mertech Control and Instrumentation Panel. The gas engines are capable of operation with a methane content of gas as low as 25 percent and for normal operation the carburation is set for a methane content of gas between 28 and 35 percent. The gas engines and associated plant are housed in self-contained I.S.O. acoustic containers.

From the compressor, gas passes at 2.7 bars to each generator set, via Preamberg filter which filters out particles to 5 microns. The electricity generated is supplied directly to M.A.N.W.E.B Sub-station which houses their switchgear.

The Methane Gas Extraction and Electricity Power Generation Plant has been designed for fail-safe operation. In addition to the safety features associated with the individual items of equipment, there is an overall safety monitoring system built into the operation of the plant.

The Scheme is designed as combined heat and power and consideration is presently being given to the use of the recoverable waste heat to produce hot water for the Festival Garden Site. It is estimated that the waste heat from the exhaust gas, engine lubricating oil and jacket cooling will yield a recoverable heat of 46.5 TJ/year initially. The temperature of the hot water from the heat exchangers will be approximately 80 degrees centigrade.

The Contractor for the Electricity Power Generation System was Messrs. Mertech Installation Services Ltd., Luton, Bedfordshire, the Caterpillar gas engines were supplied by Messrs. H. Leverton and Co. Ltd., and the Engineering and Management Consultants for the Merseyside Development Corporation are Messrs. Matan and Partners Ltd., Liverpool.

Messrs. Matan and Partners estimated the capital cost of the waste heat recovery plant of just under £250.000, making the total C.H.P. scheme of about £ 0.75 million The payback period for the Electricity Power Generation Scheme is 4 years and for the waste heat recovery scheme, the payback period is less than 3 years. The total cost combined heat and power (C.H.P.) will have a payback period of about 3 years.

The electricity power generation scheme using the low calorific value landfill methane gas is the first of its kind in the U.K. The technical expertise are now available and it is hoped that this successful scheme can be repeated at other landfill sites in the U.K. and landfill and sewage gas can now be regarded as profitable instead of being associated with problems. In 1981 when the Merseyside Development Corporation began the task of transforming the Otterspool site into a beautiful landscaped environment, the methane gas from the refuse tip was regarded as a major environmental problem. Innovation and inventiveness has now transformed this into a major success story.

6 ECONOMICS

Gas utilisation options are affected by the fluctuation in energy price and we are continuously reviewing the economics of various options. The falling price of natural gas has forced down the price of landfill gas and many schemes involving the direct sale of landfill gas have been put in abeyance pending possible fuel price recovery. At present and in the immediate future, we believe that electricity power generation will be the best commercially viable proposition.

For the project at the International Garden Festival site, the projected net income is £176000, £157000, £15700, £126000 and £106000 in year 1 to year 5 respectively and £638000 in years 6 to 12. This site can not be regarded as typical for landfill gas utilisation because of the priority given to environmental control. A typical site capable of yielding 100TJ per year of gas would provide the following:

Power generated   1.0MW
Waste Heat   1.8MW (available)
Capital Costs:
Power Generation   = £550000
Gas Extraction   = £200000
Income (electricity)= £230000/year
Operating Cost   = £80000/year

The cost of the gas collection system would depend on the surface area of the landfill site. A site with a depth of 10 metres or deeper is more economical. Income from the sale of electricity to the Electricity Board at 2.7 pence per KWhr is considerably less than in house use of the electricity generated. The net income from the available energy from waste heat would depend on the percentage utilisation of this source of energy.

The viability of a power generation scheme can only be assessed individually. Generally, the landfill site must be large enough (say more than 1 million tonnes of refuse) to produce sufficient gas to generate a minimum of 300 KW for in house use or 1 MW for sale to the Electricity Board. Other non-commercial considerations including environmental impact such as methane gas migration control, odour nuisance, vegetation die-back and the need to resolve other hazardous situations can improve the viability of the gas utilisation scheme if the cost of gas extraction is borne by these.

Economics of scale is an important factor in the viability of the power generation scheme. Schemes with 2 MW and above can generally be regarded as viable, provided the gas quantity and quality can be maintained for a period in excess of five years. The financial appraisal should take cognizance of the fact that on a completed landfill site, gas production would decrease exponentially and this could affect the income in subsequent years. On the other hand, sites which are still being filled could make up the decrease in gas production and may even contribute to an increase in gas production during the filling period. The quality of gas is also very important. It is important that gas analysis should be undertaken before embarking on any landfill gas power generation. Landfill gas contains traces of hydrocarbons contaminants. At certain levels, the gas may require to be treated before being fed into the gas engine or turbine. The cost of this could affect the viability of the project. From the foregoing, it is apparent that the economics of landfill gas power generation is very complex. Technical evaluation and investment appraisal should be carried out for an individual scheme. For the scheme to be regarded as viable, the payback period should be less than 5 years. However, the net present value or internal rate of return method of economic appraisal is more appropriate for this type of project than the payback period method.

Fig 1   Methane gas power station

Fig 2   Generation plant

Fig 3

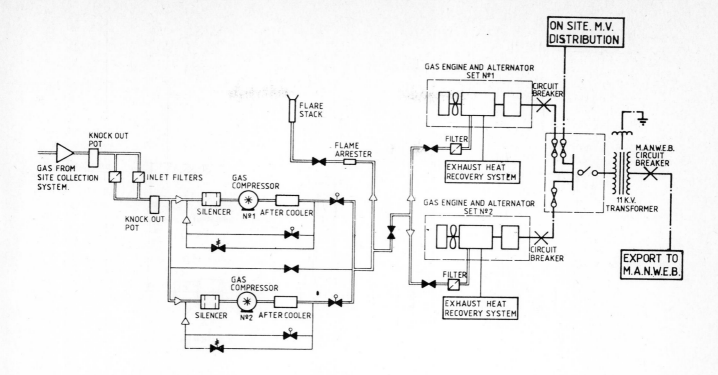

Fig 4   Landfill methane gas utilization electricity power generation scheme

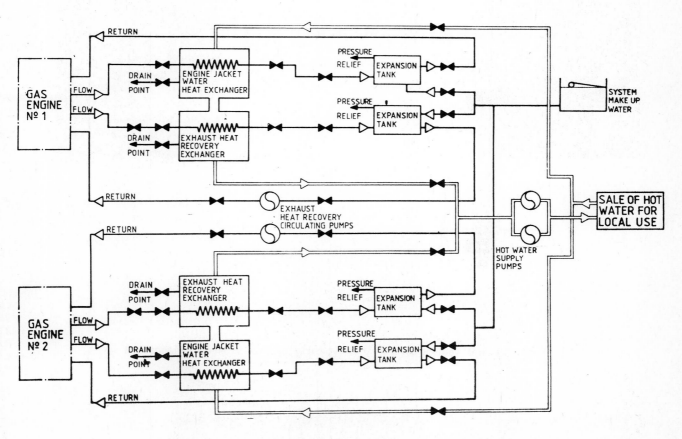

Fig 5   Landfill methane gas utilization waste heat recovery scheme

C07/88

A comparison of the economics of using biogas for heating, electricity generation or vehicle propulsion

D J PICKEN, MA, PhD, CEng, FIMechE, MIProdE
School of Mechanical and Production Engineering, Leicester Polytechnic, Leicester

SYNOPSIS   Biogas is always produced when anaerobic digestion is used to treat organic waste such as sewage sludge, animal slurry from intensive farming or vegetable waste.   Since the gas is about 65% methane its energy content is considerable (25 MJ/m^3) and apparent energy savings are very desirable.   However, there are economic penalties in the form of capital costs, maintenance and operational convenience.

The paper discusses the technology of using the gas in boilers, spark ignition and diesel engines, both stationary with heat recovery and in vehicles, and the relative costs of each.

The technical and practical problems which arose during a project to convert a fleet of vehicles to operate on sewage gas are described.

A comparison of the different uses is made in terms of location of the gas source, costs of treatment such as compressing and scrubbing and payback time for each application.

1 INTRODUCTION

Biogas is always produced when anaerobic digestion is used to treat organic waste such as sewage sludge, animal slurry from intensive farming, or vegetable waste.   It can also be produced from landfill operations of municipal waste, though in this case it may have a rather low methane content (less than 50%).   More normally biogas has a constitution of about 65% methane, 34% CO_2 and some trace elements of which the most important is hydrogen sulphide.

Typically the energy content is 25 MJ/m^3 and gas is given off a mesophyllic anaerobic digester at 1 to 2 cubic metres per day per cubic metre of digester size.   Retention time can vary from 8 days to 25 days depending on the waste and the degree of treatment required.

The quantity of energy available in biogas is appreciable, but, like all forms of energy, its conversion to heat, work or electrical energy depends on the economics of conversion and use.

The gas can be used for water and/or space heating, as a fuel source for an engine to produce mechanical or electrical work or to distribute energy outside the site, either as compressed gas or piped to nearby energy users. The decision on the use of the gas is dependant on (i) the need for a particular form of energy (ii) the complexity and cost of installing and maintaining the system and (iii) the savings achieved by replacing the alternative energy source to the site.

2 BIOGAS FOR HEATING

Any potential source of biogas should be considered in terms of use for water heating, space heating or process heating.   Burners for this use need be very little different from those used for natural gas except that jet sizes are increased to allow for the lower energy density of the fuel due to the carbon dioxide content.

If hydrogen sulphide is present it can be removed by scrubbing, or allowed for by replacing copper-based components in contact with the gas.   It is also advisable to remove waste gases at a temperature above the dew point or to use a non-reactive liner to the flue to prevent sulphuric acid attack.   Environmental considerations may dictate removal of hydrogen sulphide before burning.

Some proportion (up to 50%) of the heat may be required to keep the digester at its required temperature, say 35°C for a mesophyllic system.

3 BIOGAS FOR ELECTRICITY GENERATION

3.1 General Considerations

The second most common use for biogas is its use as a fuel for an internal combustion engine. The engine can sometimes be used directly to supply mechanical power to a pump or compressor, but is more usually attached to an alternator. This allows power to be distributed further from the biogas source (e.g. throughout a sewage works) or, if an asynchronous generator is used, to be distributed further afield via the Electricity Board lines.   The economics of this latter operation will be dependent on the terms available from the Electricity Board.

One advantage of using an engine is that heat recovery can be applied. This will at least supply all the energy required to heat the digester without decreasing the electrical output. It may even provide all the water and space heating that can be used on site.

Since the energy density of biogas is relatively low, storage at low pressure occupies a large volume and is thus unlikely to be economic. Thus the engine should be operated continuously to use the gas at approximately the rate at which the gas is generated. This, of course, assumes that electricity demand is approximately constant, which is fairly unlikely on a limited site such as a farm. The likelihood of a heat energy demand which is continuously proportional to the electricity demand is even more remote. Thus the economic returns are unlikely to be as great as is suggested by the energy the system can produce, and cannot be calculated without detailed information on the individual site energy requirements.

Capital investment is also likely to be affected by requirements for standby power. If failure of the electrical supply cannot be tolerated on site, then either a second engine generator set must be available or it must be possible to use the mains supply as a back-up. In this latter case the digester heating requirement must be met by a standby boiler. In the event of a failure of the biogas supply, an alternative fuel or energy supply must be available.

3.2 Types of Engine for use with Biogas

Either spark ignition engines or dual-fuel engines may be used with biogas. Because of the relatively low demand, such engines are usually modifications of engines designed for other fuels; and in the case of smaller systems, of automotive engines.

Before operating on biogas, both types of engine will require modifications to the valves and valve seats. Because of the 'dry' nature of biogas there is no lubricating property in the fuel and these components will need modifying to a material which is more resistant to wear than normal. Some manufacturers also add additional lubrication to the valves for an engine operating on any gaseous fuel.

Biogas, as produced or after 'scrubbing' to methane, cannot easily be liquefied. It has therefore to be introduced to both types of engine by means of a carburettor and is present during the compression stroke.

3.3 Spark ignition engines

Can be cheap if based on automotive engines.
Efficiency of about 25% at full load, falling off rapidly at part load.
Can operate on 100% biogas with no supplementary fuel.
Fuel can be replaced by gasoline or propane provided that additional carburettors are fitted.
No danger of knocking provided that compression ratio is below about 10:1.

No engine modifications required from gasoline version other than gas carburettor and hardened valves and valve seats.
Normally used on farm biogas units and increasingly on larger systems.

Compression ignition engines

Often used on larger (municipal sewage) systems.
Efficiency of 30 to 35% throughout the load range.
Requires a minimum of 7% of total fuel to be supplied as diesel oil.
Can operate on all ratios of biogas/diesel oil from 93:7 to 0:100 - very desirable when biogas production fluctuates.

To achieve the above conditions several major modifications are necessary, e.g. lower compression ratios than conventional diesels, provision of extra cooling to injectors, fitting of gas carburettor, valve modifications as for spark ignition engines.
Automotive diesel engines generally require much more than 7% diesel oil - often as much as 50%.

4 BIOGAS FOR VEHICLE PROPULSION

The use of biogas as a fuel for road vehicles is not new. It was used at Mogden sewage treatment works, London from 1942 to 1968, and has been considered, and used, elsewhere since.

The concept of increasing the energy density of biogas by compression or liquefaction is attractive. It removes the need to use the fuel as it is produced and, in theory widens the geographical area in which the fuel can be used, hence enabling use to be balanced with supply.

Disadvantages include (i) the cost of compression or liquefaction and the associated plant, (ii) the cost of vehicle modification, (iii) the fact that the compressed or liquefied biogas is still relatively low in energy density when the fuel containers are taken into account, and (iv) the lack of a countrywide network of filling stations which would make it necessary for any vehicle to have the capacity to revert to operation on conventional liquid fuel if it ventured far from base.

A case study of this application of biogas is presented below, in which most of the technical problems are described.

5 OPERATION OF LIGHT VANS AND DIESEL TANKERS ON BIOGAS AT COLCHESTER SEWAGE TREATMENT WORKS

5.1 Description of Colchester Sewage Treatment Works

The works at Colchester treat the sewage and industrial wastes from a town of 105 000 population. Approximately 7500 cubic metres of sewage per day is conveyed by a gravity flow sewerage system to works providing primary settlement followed by biological filtration and secondary settlement, and 15 000 cubic metres per day is received via a low level pumping station for primary settlement followed by biological oxidation by the activated sludge process using surface aeration. Primary and secondary sludges from the two plants are collected in consolidation tanks and augmented by primary sludge from a number of rural works thus bringing the total contributing population to 155 000. The consolidated mixed sludge, which amounts to 250 cubic metres per day is then treated by anaerobic digestion at a temperature of $28-30^{\circ}C$. for an average retention period of 19 days. Gas produced in this process averages 3 700 cubic metres per day and comprises 65% methane, 34% carbon dioxide and traces of other gases, the most significant of which is hydrogen sulphide, approximately 0.1%. This biogas, supplemented by diesel fuel was used for electricity generation to meet on-site power requirements, but on carefully costing this operation it was found by the late 1970s to compare unfavourably with the purchase from the public supply and thus, in January 1980 power generation was abandoned and the generating plant relegated to a stand-by role.

The uses of biogas before 1980 and the proposed uses after 1980 are illustrated in Figure 1.

5.2 Technical details

It was estimated that after satisfying the heat demand of the digestion process and providing space heating for offices and workshops there would be a surplus of at least 1200 cubic metres of biogas per day, which unless a use could be found for it would have to be flared off.

A number of possible uses, such as selling to the National Gas Council, direct sale as fuel to industry or sale of the purified gas as industrial methane were considered but the most attractive and readily available outlet appeared to be as fuel for the fleet of petrol and diesel driven vehicles based on site.

The vehicles based on or regularly calling at Colchester Sewage Treatment Works comprised 12 light petrol driven vans having engine capacities between 1 and 2.5 litres, 2 sludge tankers with diesel engines of 8.5 litres capacity and 2 sludge tankers with diesel engines of 14 litres capacity. The fuel consumption of this fleet was approximately 100 litres of petrol and 200 litres of diesel fuel per day. Information available at that time indicated that 1 litre of petrol could be replaced by 0.75 cubic metres of methane. If methane could be used as replacement to all petrol and diesel for this fleet, 225 cubic metres of methane or 350 cubic metres of biogas per day, would be the likely requirement. Clearly, there was more than enough surplus gas to supply this fleet.

The following items were investigated:-

1. The provision of a plant to produce gas in the form most suitable for use in road vehicles.

2. The conversion of petrol engines to methane fuel.

3. The conversion of diesel engines to methane fuel.

Before these investigations could be progressed very far, a decision had to be taken as to the most suitable form of the gas and it was accepted from the outset that to obtain maximum use of storage capacity and to give a clean burning fuel, the bulk of the carbon dioxide and hydrogen sulphide must first be removed. The possibility of doing this by chemical absorption or by extraction with organic solvents with subsequent solvent recovery was investigated, but it became apparent that with a plentiful supply of water (final effluent) the simplest and most economical method would be scrubbing with water under pressure. The enriched gas so produced could then be carried on the vehicles in low pressure containers, high pressure cylinders or as a liquid.

Low pressure containers would be extremely bulky and were ruled out for this reason, and despite the availability of aluminium cylinders, storage at high pressure would significantly reduce the pay load of the smaller vehicles. Liquefaction required complex plant, would be expensive to maintain and the constant 'boil off' of gas to maintain cryogenic conditions appeared to present problems which might require expensive solution.

There was, therefore, no ideal solution, but of the three possibilities, high pressure storage was preferred although the possibility of cryogenic storage, which would facilitate the transport of gas to other vehicle bases, was felt to warrant further investigation at a later date.

The following plant specification was then decided upon.

1. To be capable of processing up to 1200 cubic metres of biogas per day.

2. To remove carbon dioxide by scrubbing with water under pressure.

3. To yield an end product of not less than 95% methane.

4. To discharge the product into vehicle cylinders at pressures up to 189 bar.

A number of manufacturers were invited to submit prices for such a plant, and Bristol Pneumatics Ltd., a British Company, quoted for 3 x 400 cubic metre modules to meet the specified capacity. An order was placed with this manufacturer for one module, i.e. of 400 cubic metre capacity.

The conversion of petrol engines to run on methane is well established and kits are available "off the shelf".

Additional experience has accrued and conversion equipment developed from the operation of engines fuelled by Liquid Petroleum Gas (L.P.G.) and such equipment preceded by an additional pressure reducing valve may be used.

There was very little information available on the operation of automotive diesel engines on methane but preliminary investigations revealed that up to one third of the diesel fuel might be replaced by gas with only minor modifications to the engine.

The conversion of both types of engine is discussed more fully below.

5.3 Description of plant

The plant shown diagramatically in Fig. 2 comprises four main units as follows:-

A compressor

A "scrubber" for the removal of unwanted gases.

A high pressure storage unit.

A vehicle filling tower.

Biogas from the digesters is fed to the first two stages of the four stage compressor and from there passes to the scrubber at a pressure of approximately 13 bar. In the scrubber the gas is subjected to counter current washing with water at a mean pressure of 10 bar and then returned to stages 3 and 4 of the compressor from which it is discharged to the high pressure store at a controlled maximum pressure of 240 bar. Stored gas is decanted into the vehicle cylinders on demand via the filling tower.

The compressor has a rated suction capacity of 30.5 cubic metres per hour and is driven by an 11 kW flame-proof motor which also drives a fan providing an air blast for the inter-stage coolers. Moisture separators are included in the gas input line and between stages, the latter being drained to a sequential "dump block" from which, at predetermined intervals, the collected moisture is discharged. The unit normally operates automatically although there is also provision for "hand" operation. In the automatic mode the unit is controlled by the pressure in the storage cylinders, switching off when the maximum safe working pressure of 240 bar is reached and re-starting when the pressure drops to 210 bar. The safety of the unit and of personnel is ensured by the inclusion of pressure control valves and pressure release valves at all potentially dangerous points.

The compressor, motor and controlgear is housed in a weatherproof cabinet which makes the provision of any further housing unnecessary.

The scrubber comprises a steel cylinder which provides a water seal and an absorption chamber filled with random plastic packing. Gas from stage 2 of the compressor enters the bottom of the absorption chamber and passes up through the packing where it is brought into contact with the water which enters the top of the chamber via a spray head. Sewage effluent (15 mq/l B.O.D., 25mg/1 S.S.) provides the absorption water which is fed into the system by a multi-stage pump providing up to 10 cubic metres per hour. The pump is driven by a 7.5 kw motor. After use the water is returned to the sewage treatment works via the site drainage. The water seal is maintained by a level control valve which allows the flow of water to be varied between 4 and 10 cubic metres per hour, the flow being controlled at any predetermined rate by pneumatic valves actuated by scrubbed gas.

The high pressure store consists of a bank of 9 steel cylinders each of 70 litres water capacity and a maximum safe working pressure of 240 bar. The bank of cylinders is sub-divided into three banks of three which are interconnected on both the inlet and discharge side by a cascade valve system which automatically ensures that on entering the store, gas passes first to the bank of cylinders which is at the highest pressure. When this bank is fully charged the gas is passed to the bank at the next highest pressure and finally to the bank at lowest pressure. When gas leaves the store it does so in the reverse order. This system increases the effective available capacity of the store and allows faster filling of the vehicle cylinders than would be possible if all storage cylinders were discharging simultaneously.

The filling tower provides two vehicle fuelling points. Each point has a flexible hose fitted with a "snap on" connector and is controlled by a three way valve having "off", "vent" and "fill" positions, the "vent" position being required to depressurise the line before disconnecting. The system is also provided with a pressure control valve to limit the filling pressure to the safe working pressure of the vehicle cylinders and a pressure gauge to indicate actual cylinder pressure. The quantity of gas transferred is calculated from the pressures at the beginning and end of the operation.

5.4 Engine Modifications

Spark ignition vehicles

The modification of these vehicles was essentially very similar to the well-known technology for using Liquid Petroleum Gas (L.P.G.). Each vehicle was fitted with one or two 31.5 litre, 189 bar methane cylinders, each holding the equivalent of 9 litres of petrol.

Methane was taken from these through a pressure reducing valve and a "normally closed" solenoid valve to a pressure regulator and gas carburettor. This gas carburettor was placed in series between the air filter and the normal petrol carburettor, so that the throttle valve for the latter also controlled the methane and air flow through the gas carburettor. A single switch was fitted on the driver's console to select either methane or petrol, but not both.

Power output was essentially unchanged by the switchover, except for a slight decrease in maximum power when methane is used, due to the decrease in volumetric efficiency caused by the loss of mixture cooling due to evaporation in the carburettor. It was also noted that methane, like L.P.G., would not provide any lubrication to the engine valves and seats. This lubrication is normally provided by the lead additives in petrol. For this reason vehicles were modified according to standard L.P.G. practice by fitting hardened valves and valveseats. The system is shown diagrammatically in Fig.3.

Diesel engined tanker

It was decided from the outset that the technology was not available for injecting the methane into the engine after the compression stroke. Therefore, it was necessary to introduce the methane into the inlet air in the same manner as in the spark ignition engine, retaining the diesel pump and injector to provide ignition and the greater portion of the energy.

Calculations indicated that it should be possible to compress mixtures of methane and air up to a limit of about 50% stoichiometric ratio at the compression ratios employed, before pre-combustion became a real danger. This compares with a maximum fuel/air ratio using diesel oil of about 90% stoichiometric for this type of engine. Thus the limit to substitution should be about 55% of the energy supplied by methane, and 45% supplied by diesel oil.

However the financial limitations imposed on the project did not allow an engine to be bench-tested with full instrumentation to detect the onset of detonation and thus it was decided to aim for a more conservative substitution ratio. Obviously if this aim was too low, there would be too little economic advantage in saving diesel oil. It was therefore decided to compromise on a substitution of 30% of diesel oil by methane. This, it was decided, would give an appreciable saving in diesel oil, while allowing the lorry to operate for a full day on 3 or 4 cylinders of methane, which could be conveniently attached to the chassis. The 70% maximum output available from diesel oil only would also be sufficient to enable the lorry to return to base if the methane cylinders ran out during a journey.

A further complication for vehicle diesel engines as opposed to diesel generating sets was the need to operate at varying speeds as well as varying loads.

The modifications carried out to the engine to meet these aims were:

(i) The fuel pump maximum delivery was reduced to 70% normal operating maximum.

(ii) A ten position butterfly valve was fitted as a restrictor in the engine air intake line.

(iii) An additional air intake was added to the inlet manifold and a methane carburettor, including a throttle valve attached. The size of this carburettor was decided by assuming approximately one third of the engine air flow would pass through it.

(iv) The control cable from the driver's throttle control to the fuel pump governor was extended to operate the methane carburettor throttle as well as the fuel pump governor. Thus increased power demand by the driver increased both oil and methane flow to the engines. Methane was supplied to the carburettor in exactly the same manner as for the spark ignition engines.

Initial setting up procedure included analysis of exhaust smoke and exhaust temperature. This proved to be unsatisfactory in road conditions and the eventual method chosen was to operate the lorry at full load on a rolling road dynamometer. The main air inlet

butterfly valve was then adjusted to give an acceptable level of smoke in the exhaust. This was found to be a satisfactory solution and the butterfly valve could be locked in this position for the operating life of the engine. The system is shown diagrammatically in Fig. 4.

5.5 Costs

The costs of the fuel preparation plant installed at Colchester (1981 prices) were as follows:

Scrubber	£8900
Compressor	£6700
Storage (Optional)	£6700
Fuelling dispenser	£2600
Site works	£3300
Total	£28 200

The costs of vehicle conversion are:

Petrol engined van (including 1 gas cylinder)	£400
Diesel engined tanker (including 3 gas cylinders)	£550

Unfortunately the project was never brought to its full potential as changes in operating requirements reduced the number of vehicles which could be modified, and thus biogas usage never matched the potential output of the scrubbing and compressing plant. The project was finally abandoned in 1985.

6 COMPARATIVE ECONOMICS OF THE ALTERNATIVE USES OF BIOGAS

There is no absolute measure of the value of biogas. In every application its value must be obtained from the cost of the fuel which it replaces. This latter cost will vary from one area to another and will certainly vary with time. Thus any comparison can only be relative and each individual system will need to be analysed using the costs prevailing at that place and time.

The following assumptions have been made in producing Figs. 5 & 6.

(i) The digester system has been built with the object of treating waste material: thus the digester cost is not capital expenditure to be paid for by biogas utilisation.

(ii) Engine generator sets with associated control gear and heat recovery cost £300 per kilowatt capacity installed.

(iii) Boiler systems cost £20 per kW installed and are 70% efficiency.

(iv) Compression and scrubbing equipment for vehicle is £15,000 for an installation which will supply 100 kW equivalent of gas.

(v)   Vehicle fuel costs 80 p/gallon (before tax) and the vehicles are 20% efficient.

(vi)   Heating may be compared with off peak electricity prices at say 1.5 p/kWh.

(vii)   Electricity generation is worth 2.5p/kWh and the engine and generator is 25% efficient.

Then if we consider 100 kW equivalent rate of biogas production (about 100 m^3 of digester volume):

A boiler could produce 70kW of heat energy
       i.e. 105 p/h.
The electric power generated would be 25 kW
       i.e. 62.5 p/h.
To this can be added, say, 50 kW of heating from waste heat recovery
       i.e. 50 x 1.5 = 75 p/h
             making a total of 137.5 p/h.
Liquid fuel (either diesel fuel or petrol) input to vehicles will be 100 kW or approximately 2.2 gall/h at 80 p/gallon
       i.e. 154 p/h.

7 CONCLUSION

    The simple analysis shown above can only be used as an indicator.   For any given site there is a limit to the amount of any one type of energy that can be used effectively and thus a combination of uses may be the only available method of using a large amount of biogas.

Further, energy costs can vary greatly with time and with location of the site (particularly from one country to another).

The final decision for economic use of the gas will also be affected by considerations of the simplicity of capital equipment and of operation.   Thus a user is likely to choose as priorities:

(i)   Heating, if sufficient gas can be profitably used.

(ii)   Combined heat and power if:
(a) either the electricity can be used on site, or advantageous terms can be arranged with the electricity board, and,
(b) a reasonable proportion of the heat can be used on site.

(iii)   Automotive fuel.   This however will be very dependant on the base cost of fuel oil.   Its advantage will be increased when the world supply of oil starts to decrease and prices rise.

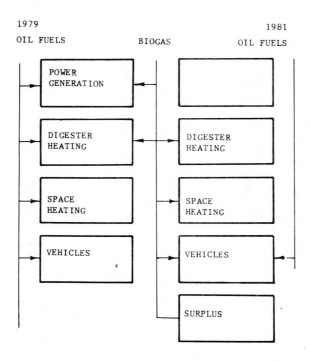

Fig 1   Usage of biogas and oil fuels showing proposed changes at Colchester sewage works

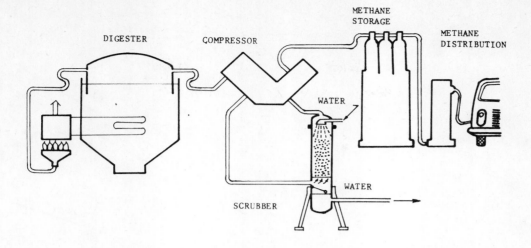

Fig 2   Line diagram of methane plant for automotive use

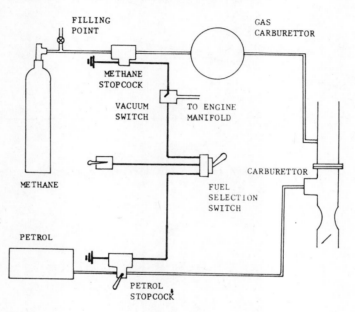

Fig 3   Conversion of a petrol engine to use either methane or petrol

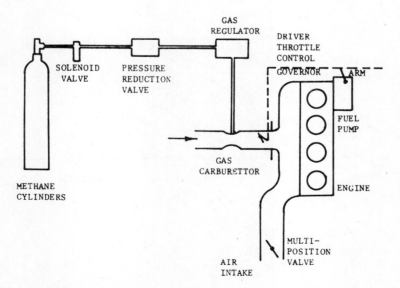

Fig 4   Conversion of a diesel engine to operate with 30 per cent methane
         substitution

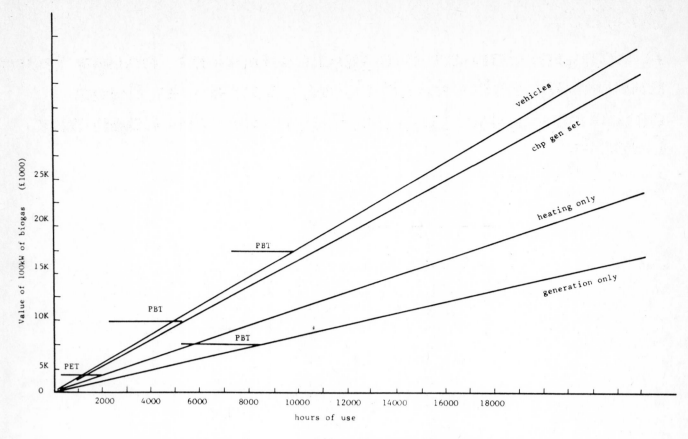

Fig 5   Income from biogas operating hours, indicating pay-back times (PBT)

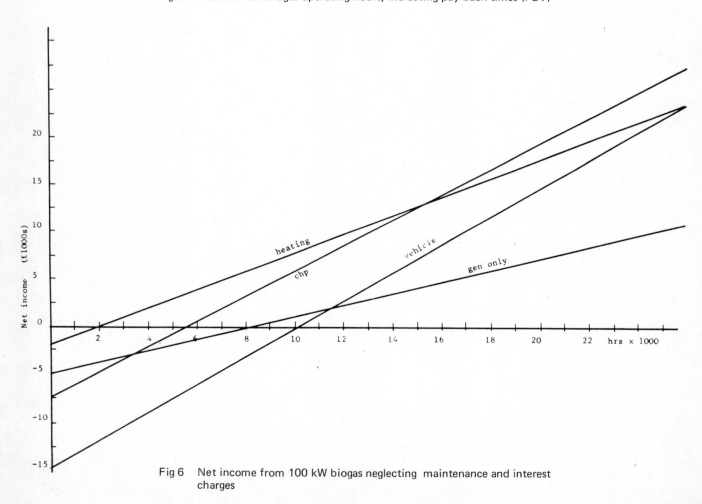

Fig 6   Net income from 100 kW biogas neglecting maintenance and interest charges

A comparison of the application of 'enegy from municipal solid waste' technology in three countries — the United Kingdom, Sweden and Canada

A A KROL, BSc, PhD and **C G DENT**, BA, MSc
Harwell Laboratory, Oxfordshire

SYNOPSIS   The UK, Sweden and Canada are participants in an International Energy Agency programme designed to co-ordinate R&D activity on energy from waste (EFW) technologies. The scope and content of the individual national R&D programmes are a direct result of the different institutional, economic and environmental factors which govern application of such technologies in each country. A description of these factors is given together with an assessment of their influence in shaping the existing and likely future role of landfill gas, refuse derived fuel and mass incineration in each country.

1.   INTRODUCTION

Since 1986 the UK, Sweden and Canada have been participants in an International Energy Agency programme (Task IV of the IEA Biomass Energy Agreement) aimed at establishing and organising co-operative research and development on technical and environmental aspects of energy recovery from municipal wastes. The organisation leading and co-ordinating activity under this programme is the Environmental Safety Centre at Harwell Laboratory.

During the past year three reports have been issued detailing research and development activity in each of the three countries (1,2,3). In addition a fourth report has been produced which summarises the research effort in each country and provides a detailed analysis of further R&D needs and the scope for collaborative and complementary research activity(4). These reports are the source of material for this paper and contain extensive bibliographies.

In general, the co-operation programme has been focused on technical issues relevant to energy from waste (EFW) technologies. However, it was recognised at an early stage that the application of the various EFW technologies, and in turn the direction of R&D activity, was very much a product of the different institutional, economical, geographical and environmental 'climates' in each country. The purpose of this paper is to give an outline of these factors (summarised in Table 1).

An additional aim of the paper is to promote discussion on the potential benefits of EFW processes to the UK, and as a result an emphasis has been placed on description of environmental and economic aspects.

For a more detailed description of the R&D programmes of the individual countries (of which a summary is given in Table 2), and our suggestions for future collaboration, the reader is referred to the four reports referenced earlier.

2.   EFW OPTIONS

The application of EFW technologies is intimately linked with the overall waste management decision making process. Figure 1 is an attempt to formalise the decision framework for uptake of EFW technologies. The route taken within any country in moving through this network is a function of the energy from waste "climate" which exists there. Figure 1 may also be regarded as a flowsheet for MSW processing. The efficiency and characteristics of any given process have implications for all subsequent downstream processes in the route towards waste disposal and energy production. Hence, separate collection (or source grouping) of the paper fraction of municipal solid waste (MSW) affects the total potential energy yield. Similarly, separate collection of batteries will reduce emissions of heavy metals (including mercury) from thermal EFW processes.

The technologies included in Figure 1 are those which make up the MSW energy conversion options currently in use or under study in the UK, Sweden and Canada. Of these, the most important technologies in terms of current application are those involving the recovery of energy (in the form of process heat, steam, hot water and/or electricity) from one of the following processes:

o   **Mass Incineration:** the process of waste combustion in an 'as received' state.

o   **Refuse Derived Fuel (RDF) Production and Combustion:** the mechanical processing of MSW to separate a fraction of higher calorific value for subsequent combustion

(in one of many possible combuster
designs). Minimal processing (e.g.
shredding and metals removal) yields
'coarse' RDF whereas further processing to
obtain a fraction rich in paper and
plastics yields 'fluff' RDF. This may in
turn be compressed to form 'pelletised'
RDF.

o **Landfill Gas:** the production of combustible gas within landfills as a result of
microbial degradation of the organic
fraction of the landfilled waste.

Looking at the three countries as a whole,
energy from waste R&D effort reflects the above
major areas of technology application. Nevertheless, R&D work has also been identified in
other areas which have not yet reached the
commercial stage, such as pyrolysis, gasification and anaerobic digestion of MSW.

Specific R&D programmes are very dependent
on the existing and emerging EFW technologies
within each country. The pattern of uptake of
these technologies is in turn dependent on many
factors, not least the form in which the energy
is produced (e.g. hot water, steam, electricity, CHP) and the marketplace for such
energy. These factors are discussed later.

3. APPLICATION OF EFW TECHNOLOGY

3.1 Integration of Waste and Energy Management

MSW can be considered as a waste requiring
disposal and/or as a resource in terms of its
material and energy content. The extent to
which it is viewed as the latter differs within
each country, for a number of reasons. Of
particular importance are the quite different
national energy balances which exist in each
country and the pressures to seek alternative
supplies of energy in order to meet demand. In
Sweden such pressures are particularly acute as
a result of three factors:

o The total quantity of electricity generated
by hydro power (currently 50% of the total)
is expected to remain constant because of
restrictions on further development.

o It is planned to phase out nuclear power
(which currently produces most of the non-
hydro generated electricity) by the year
2010.

o Sweden has only limited availability of
indigenous fuels, mainly wood and peat.

As a result, Sweden has placed particular
emphasis on exploitation of alternative sources
of energy, including EFW. By contrast the UK,
with oil, coal and gas reserves and a continuing nuclear power programme, and Canada,
with cheap hydro and nuclear power in addition
to abundant fossil fuel reserves, are not
subject to the same pressures.

Sweden is fortunate in having had a long-
term positive policy in favour of the introduction and use of district heating networks,
which in 1985 accounted for 10% of the final
end use of energy(2). The existence of 'hot
water' district heating provides a ready
market for any locally produced fuel, such as
MSW, and enables better use of low grade heat,
particuarly if the EFW facility fulfils the
base load needs of such a system. In the UK
there is no national policy on district
heating networks although they have been
established by certain local authorities.
Canada also has no significant district
heating schemes.

In terms of electricity generation, the
UK government has acted to aid private
producers of electricity by obliging regional
electricity distribution authorities (the area
boards) to buy electricity from any source at
a 'reasonable' price (1983 Energy Act). This
has created an enhanced potential marketplace for EFW processes. Although we are not
aware of similar legislation in Sweden, the
pressures on the electricity distributors to
seek alternative supplies mean that in
practice they are willing to co-operate with
operators of facilities operating CHP
processes. Canada has no such legislation.

The factors outlined above have combined
to ensure that Sweden converts much more of
its MSW arisings to energy than either the UK
or Canada. Over 60% of Swedish MSW is subject
to thermal energy recovery operations(2) (i.e.
mass incineration or RDF production) whilst in
the UK and Canada the figure is less than
10%(1,3).

3.2 Landfill Gas

Taking the three countries as a whole, landfill remains the major disposal option for
MSW. In the UK, over 90% of MSW is land-
filled(1). In terms of the production and
utilisation of landfill gas the UK is the
market leader of the three countries, with
approximately 5% of the recently estimated
economic potential of the resource (10,000
GWhr/yr) currently being extracted(1). Sweden
extracts a similar percentage of its smaller
landfill gas resource (1000-1500 GWhr/yr)(2)
whilst in Canada there are very few landfill
gas abstraction schemes (most landfills are
too small and remote for cost-effective
operations)(3).

One reason for the great reliance within
the UK on landfill for disposal of MSW is that
on a national scale there is a net annual
generation of void space (see Section 5.3).
Despite this, there are local shortages,
particularly around some of the major cities.
A similar situation exists close to the large
Canadian cities. In Sweden there is a
relative shortage of landfill space and a
genuine measure of environmental concern at

both public and government level over landfill as a major disposal route.

Industrial boilers and kilns are the major users of landfill gas in the UK although there are also schemes involving greenhouse heating and electricity generation. The latter use is seen to offer potential for 'remote' landfills. Most of the gas abstracted in Swedish schemes is used to provide heat for district heating networks.

3.3 Mass Incineration

Mass incineration with heat recovery (for district heating) is used as a disposal route for 50% of all MSW arisings in Sweden(2). In contrast, incineration is a minor disposal route (less than 10% of all arisings) in both the UK(1) and Canada(3) and in these countries many existing incinerators do not operate with heat recovery. Two of the major problems are finding a ready market for the energy produced (in the absence of the district heating networks which exist in many Swedish cities) and matching supply to demand i.e. ensuring as much as possible of the useful energy produced is sold. These problems are largely overcome when the energy is sold in the form of electricity, but the thermodynamic efficiency in this case is much reduced (unless when part of a CHP scheme). Even when an economic case **can** be made for mass incineration and energy recovery there can be major problems, certainly within the UK, of raising the necessary capital involved. The scope for public sector financing is restricted because of the imposed limits on borrowing, even if incineration may be a cost effective investment, and the private sector remains substantially unconvinced of the commercial viability of incineration in the UK.

Swedish mass incinerators supply 5% of the total energy demand of the countries district heating networks(2) and usually operate in providing for 'base load' energy requirements. This is almost the sole use of heat from mass incinerators although one plant (in Stockholm) does operate as a CHP station. Where district heating networks do exist in the UK, mass incinerators have also operated with varying degrees of success in supplying heat (e.g. Sheffield, Nottingham and Mansfield). Elsewhere, the lack of such a network has resulted in energy being recovered as process heat (Coventry), or electricity without combined heat recovery (Edmonton).

In Canada, those mass incinerators with energy recovery all supply steam to industrial or commercial users.

3.4 Refuse Derived Fuel (RDF)

RDF (in one or more of its forms i.e. coarse, fluff and pelletised) is manufactured and utilised in all three countries, although only Sweden has experience of all three.

Approximately 10% of all Swedish MSW is processed in separation plants(2), the majority of which were built in the 5 year period 1977-1982 with the primary aim of materials recovery. In this role they were essentially a failure, primarily as a result of difficulties in marketing the materials produced. Some of these plants have since been adapted to RDF production. Recent plants (for coarse, fluff and pelletised RDF manufacture) have been almost exclusively devoted to this role. In Sweden the main market for RDF is seen as the district heating network. The main potential advantages of the fuel over unprocessed waste are that it can be manufactured throughout the year for use during periods of peak heating demand in the winter, and it is more suitable for use in small district heating plants. Currently RDF is burnt in a wide variety of facilities e.g. grate furnaces (pelletised, fluff and coarse), bubbling fluidised beds (coarse) and circulating fluidised beds (fluff).

In the UK, the development of pelletised RDF production facilities has, to a large extent, been in response to the potential market which exists in supplying the fuel to industrial solid fuel boilers. Nevertheless, commercial applications remain limited. A major problem remains one of marketing the product. Consumer resistance persists as a result of both actual and perceived technical problems in its utilisation.

There is no experience of pelletised RDF manufacture in Canada and production of fluff RDF at the experimental facility in Toronto has been terminated. Current experience appears confined to the production and burning of coarse RDF at the SWARU incinerator in Hamilton, Ontario (2 x 270 tonnes/day), from which electricity is produced and sold to the grid.

4. ENVIRONMENTAL FACTORS INFLUENCING EFW DEVELOPMENT

4.1 Landfill Gas

There are a number of potential environmental issues which relate to the landfilling of MSW, for example:

o   contamination of aquifers or surface waters by leachate migration;
o   migration of landfill gas and resulting potential explosion hazards;
o   trace pollutants in landfill gas.

These issues relate to the landfill operation itself rather than directly to landfill gas utilisation. In fact, the introduction of a landfill gas extraction scheme may in certain circumstances be necessary <u>to prevent</u> gas migration. Furthermore work in the UK(1), and to a lesser extent Sweden(2), suggests combustion of the extracted gas destroys many of the trace organic compounds present. Hence, the major environmental issues which may influence development of landfill gas as an EFW option relate not so much to gas extraction and utilisation itself (indeed, this may be seen as reducing the environmental problem), but to landfill as an option for MSW disposal. Environmental concerns over landfilling of MSW are particularly evident in Sweden. By contrast, the pressure from some environmental activists in Canada is generally in favour of retaining landfill until such a time as the combustion emission issue is resolved(3).

4.2 Mass Incineration and RDF

In terms of the major thermal EFW technologies (mass incineration or combustion of RDF), there are two major areas of environmental concern, (a) disposal of combustion residuals (b) flue gas emissions. With regard to (a), all three countries have, to a greater or lesser extent, been involved in R&D work into assessment of the potential hazards of the solid residuals (e.g. from leaching of hazardous components if the residues are being landfilled). However, this is not, at least for the present, the major issue. With regard to (b), there are three major areas of concern in terms of pollutants present in the emissions:

o   acid gases, mainly HCl;
o   heavy metals, mainly mercury and cadmium;
o   polychlorinated dibenzodioxins (PCDDs) and polychlorinated dibenzofurans (PCDFs).

In contrast to extraction and utilisation of landfill gas, the thermal technologies can be viewed as creating a potential environmental problem. Concern over emissions, particularly of "dioxins", has had a high profile in both Sweden and Canada. In the UK, such concerns have (thus far) been less evident. The nature of legislative control is also quite different in the UK where (at the time of writing) the concept of 'best practicable means' still prevails. In Sweden, fixed emission standards are written into the licence under which each plant operates. In Ontario, Canada, standards are applied for concentrations of pollutants at a "local point of impingement".

In February 1985 a moratorium was applied in Sweden on the construction of new MSW incinerators because of concern over "dioxin" emissions. (In 1985 approximately one third of total "dioxin" emissions in Sweden came from MSW incinerators.) In the following year the Minister of the Environment for Ontario in Canada also considered imposing such a moratorium for similar reasons (although this was not in the event implemented).

Both Sweden and Canada have taken action at national government level to fund major R&D programmes into emissions from MSW combustion,

in each case involving extensive collaboration between the Environment and Energy Departments of the respective countries. In terms of emissions from existing mass incinerators, UK action has been relatively limited.

The Swedish investigation (the ENA study) examined issues relating to the emissions of pollutants other than dioxins/furans and reported in the middle of 1986. The findings of this study were instrumental in the moratorium on construction being lifted in June 1986 and the introduction of new recommendations for emission standards (referred to as 'after measures' in Table 3). These recommended standards are likely to be phased in as conditions on the operating licences under which plants burning MSW or RDF operate. This action by the Swedish government has initiated considerable national activity with regard to the installation of 'advanced' flue gas treatment systems for mass incinerators and RDF combustion together with R&D in these areas.

The major Canadian R&D activity has been organised under the auspices of NITEP (National Incinerator Testing and Evaluation Programme). This activity complements past and continuing Swedish work and was originally designed to address five key areas(3):

(1)   Environmental/health impacts.
(2)   Sampling and analytical methods.
(3)   The link between combustion conditions and emissions.
(4)   Incineration and pollution control technology assessment.
(5)   Regulatory controls.

One further aim of NITEP is to develop a datalogging and control system for operation of incinerators and for use by regulatory authorities in checking compliance with emission limits.

At the time of writing (May 1986) there is no comparable level of R&D activity in the UK to that described above for Sweden and Canada, although a survey of the heavy metal and PCDD/PCDF content of stack emissions and their ground dispersal is being conducted on behalf of the UK Department of the Environment.

In the UK, flue gas treatment is limited to the use of electrostatic precipitators. This was also the case in both Sweden and Canada until recently. However, since 1985 a number of full scale treatment systems have been installed in Sweden(2). These are either 'dry' systems, in which lime is used to neutralise the acid gases and in which particulates (together with adsorbed PCDD/ PCDFs and oxidised mercury) are efficiently removed by fabric filters, or 'wet' systems, in which the condensate formed by cooling the flue gases is used to remove the pollutants. Swedish advanced flue gas treatment technology has also been evaluated in Canada as part of

NITEP(3). A 'dry' pilot-scale system, similar to that in use in Sweden, and a 'wet-dry' pilot-scale system (which uses a lime slurry) were both installed with fabric filters at the Quebec incinerator. The emission levels achieved by these systems are likely to become the standards applied to any new MSW incinerator plant in Canada. A 'wet/dry" system is to be installed at the new Vancouver plant.

In both Sweden and Canada the advanced flue gas cleaning systems in use or under evaluation have proved capable of meeting proposed emission standards for acid gases, PCDD/PCDFs and heavy metals(2,3). It is interesting to note that incinerator operators at two locations in Sweden have chosen to install more capital intensive 'wet' systems in preference to 'dry' systems. This is because the condensation of water in the flue gas allows additional low grade heat recovery, for which a market is readily available in the local district heating networks. The resultant lower net operating costs compensate for the higher capital costs of the 'wet' systems.

In Sweden measurements on plants burning RDF have also shown the need for measures to reduce flue gas emissions at such facilities(2). Pilot-scale trials are underway to determine the most appropriate technology.

The current viewpoint in both Sweden and Canada seems to be that mass incineration can be an environmentally acceptable technology, provided that combustion conditions are such as to minimise environmentally significant emissions and that a sufficiently efficient flue gas treatment system is used(4). Despite previous concerns therefore, the potential environmental impact of thermal EFW processes is not seen as a barrier to their continued or expanded use in these countries. It is interesting to speculate on whether the UK will follow the path of Sweden and Canada in investigating advanced flue gas treatment systems and regulating further on the control of emissions.

5. ECONOMIC FACTORS INFLUENCING EFW DEVELOPMENT

Table 4 provides a summary of net costs for MSW disposal in each of the three countries, by landfill alone and by each of the three major EFW technologies. International comparison of this type are notoriously difficult to make and a number of caveats need to be borne in mind when doing so. These are emphasised where appropriate.

5.1 Landfill Gas

Table 4 provides separate costs for landfill, and landfill gas recovery and utilisation. Both are important in terms of contributing to the EFW decision-making process. The cost of landfill in each country relative to other disposal options will be a major factor in

determining the total tonnage of MSW disposed of by this route and hence the total potential for energy recovery by the landfill gas option. The costs (or net profits) involved in gas recovery will in turn be a major factor in determining the development of this EFW technology at any given site.

As can be seen from Table 4, the range of costs for landfill disposal are in fact broadly similar in the UK, Sweden and Canada. However, it is important to realise that these figures do not include costs of transport, nor transfer station costs where also entailed. These have a major bearing on total costs for wastes arising in urban areas where long haul via a transfer station is the only landfill option. In the UK the quoted average unit cost of transfer station operations is £4.1/tonne and quoted transport costs (excluding those due to leasing or purchase of vehicles) vary from less than £1/tonne to over £10/tonne(1). Assuming that these additional costs are similar in Sweden and Canada, it does not seem unreasonable to place an approximate range of £5-20/tonne on the cost of using a landfill disposal route in any of the three countries, depending upon economies of scale, the use of transfer stations, and transport costs. Against this figure can be credited potential net revenues from landfill gas extraction, which are estimated to be of the order of £2.5/tonne in the UK. Thus the potential net cost of landfill disposal with gas recovery in the UK, Sweden, or Canada, is probably within the range £2.5-£17.5/tonne.

5.2 Mass Incineration and RDF

No broad similarities are apparent from Table 4 in terms of the costs in each country for mass incineration, and RDF manufacture and sale. At the time of writing, no data were available to the authors on production and combustion of RDF at the same site.

The most comprehensive analysis of the economics of running existing mass incineration and separation/composting/RDF production plants was carried out in Sweden in 1983. In this analysis no account was taken of government grants and capital costs were accounted for using the real annuity method. For each existing plant a net treatment cost was calculated by taking the difference between total treatment costs (for operation, maintenance and servicing capital) and the income received from the sale of energy or recovered materials. It is instructive to study the cost breakdowns for Swedish mass incinerators and separation/composting/RDF plants presented in Figures 2 and 3, respectively. These costs assume a real rate of interest of 4%.

For Swedish mass incineration plants operating with heat recovery and sale to district heating networks, Table 2 indicates a net average treatment cost of £3/tonne while for the 8 most successful plants Figure 2 indicates that there is a calculated average _profit_. However, Figure 2 shows that with no sale of heat the net treatment cost at these installations is £23.5/tonne, which is comparable with costs at the top end of the range quoted for the UK incinerators in Table 2 (although it should be noted that the capital and operating costs of an incinerator designed with no heat recovery would be lower than that given in Figure 2). The UK costs quoted are based on centrally collected statistics and cover the range from those incinerators operating with heat recovery, such as Sheffield (£3/tonne), to the small recently closed Rhondda incinerator which had no heat recovery (£22/tonne). The limitations of these UK cost figures shold be recognised. For instance capital servicing charges are not included; the Swedish figures presented in Figure 2 indicate that this may add an additional £4-5/tonne to the UK costs.

The costs given for Canada seem relatively high but these are based on only one set of data provided by the Province of Ontario. Energy prices are relatively cheap in Canada and this will influence the overall economics of any EFW scheme.

For Swedish separation-composting plants, Table 4 and Figure 3 indicate that there is a calculated net operating cost of £22.9/tonne although with sale of all RDF and compost produced a net cost of £4.7/tonne might be achievable. This latter figure is comparable to the expected minimum net cost of operating an RDF production plant in the UK with 100% sale of the fuel.

5.3 Influence of Economics on EFW Development In Each Country

Section 4 discussed the influence of environmental factors in shaping the 'climate' for EFW development in each country. What then are the economic factors?

The economics of mass incineration with energy recovery appear particularly favourable in Sweden when compared to those in the UK and Canada. Indeed, the figures suggest an overall _profit_ is possible. This would appear to be a major factor in explaining the greater application of this technology in Sweden and as a direct result, the much higher proportion of total energy recovery than in either the UK or Canada. The reasons are not totally clear since insufficient information is available on how costs have been calculated in the UK and Canada and hence true cost comparisons are not possible. Nevertheless, it does appear that the existence of extensive district heating networks in many Swedish cities (for which heat generated by MSW incineration can provide an all year round base load) is a major influence.

There is little RDF activity in Canada. However, cost figures for both the UK and Sweden demonstrate the potential for this EFW route in these countries. Indeed, both have substantial RDF R&D programmes to develop and demonstrate the practicality of potential markets for the fuel. In the UK this has involved a very extensive series of trials in different industrial boilers whereas in Sweden the emphasis is on the utilisation of RDF in existing and new district heating systems.

With respect to landfill gas recovery, it has been shown that the costs of _comparable_ landfill operations are broadly similar in each country. Why then is so much more MSW landfilled in the UK than in Sweden? One factor is clearly the relatively favourable economics of mass incineration in Sweden, as already discussed. Another is void space. In the UK, there is a net annual generation of voids. If local void space exists then landfill is a very economically competitive route for MSW disposal. In the UK there also appear to be fewer reservations on environmental grounds to landfill as a major disposal route. Landfill remains the cheapest option in most parts of Canada (when incinerators have been built here in recent years, one of the major aims has been in demonstrating the technology, and considerable financial support has been provided by Federal and/or Provincial Government sources).

The costs discussed above influence the total proportion of MSW landfilled in each country and, in turn, the total _potential_ for energy recovery by landfill gas. The actual development of extraction and utilisation schemes is however very dependent on both the costs of competing energy supplies and the demand for any energy produced. In Canada, most landfills are remote from potential consumers and electricity and gas prices are cheap. Hence there is little application of landfill gas technology. The UK, with high energy prices and much less remote sites is in a much better position to develop landfill gas extraction schemes. In each country there are, to a greater or lesser extent important additional factors to the favourable economics for gas extraction. These are the resultant reduction in environmental impact of the landfill and utilisation of an indigenous 'resource'.

6. FUTURE DEVELOPMENTS

Some aspects of the current individual R&D programmes in the UK, Sweden and Canada have been referred to in the above discussion. Table 2 summarises the respective national programmes. This table is a guideline to the priorities of the individual countries, and to the likely future role of the various EFW techniques in each. However, future developments will certainly remain dependent on the movement of world energy prices - a factor notoriously difficult to predict.

At present, providing that energy purchase tariffs remain favourable, it appears that the growth sectors in the UK will probably be landfill gas utilisation and RDF production and sale. In addition there may also be a role for mass incinerators and/or combined coarse RDF production and burning facilities (prepared burning) at certain locations (at the time of writing, schemes are under consideration for Liverpool (RDF) and south east London (mass incineration)). R&D on control and optimisation of flue gas emissions will probably assume a higher priority.

Sweden is also likely to make growing use of landfill gas, RDF and mass/prepared burning incinerators although with a different emphasis than in the UK (towards the latter options), because of the marketplace for low grade heat provided by district heating networks. All large Swedish thermal processing installations will be fitted with advanced flue gas cleaning systems over the next few years.

Canadian uptake of EFW technology will probably remain dominated by mass/prepared burning incinerators, with the addition of advanced flue gas cleaning systems. A limited number of additional landfill gas schemes may also be introduced.

7. INTERNATIONAL R&D COLLABORATION

From the point of view of international collaboration, the differences in emphasis between the individual EFW R&D programmes within the UK, Sweden and Canada (see Table 2) are of considerable value. They enable each country to concentrate on its own priorities while at the same time sharing in a wider R&D base. It is therefore important that results of R&D and technology assessment are 'portable' between countries. A pre-requisite for this is that such work makes use of standardised definitions, nomenclature, analytical techniques and evaluation protocol. This is a central aim of the International Energy Agency programme referred to in the Introduction. The reports issued as part of this programme have concentrated on evaluating the R&D efforts of the individual countries and suggest areas which would be valuable for collaborative ventures(1,2,3,4). The reader is referred to these for further detail.

8. AUTHORS NOTE

The views expressed in this paper are those of the authors and should not be taken as representative of those of the International Energy Agency or of the national governments of the UK, Sweden and Canada.

This work was financed by agencies of the three national governments.

REFERENCES

(1) DENT, C and KROL, A A (1987). Municipal Solid Waste Conversion to Energy: A Summary of Current Research and Development Activity in the United Kingdom. Harwell Report (available through HMSO).

(2) KROL, A A and DENT, C (1987). Municipal Solid Waste Conversion to Energy: A Summary of Current Research and Development Activity in Sweden. Harwell Report (available through HMSO).

(3) DENT, C and KROL, A A (1987). Municipal Solid Waste Conversion to Energy: A Summary of Current Research and Development Activity in Canada. Harwell Report (available through HMSO).

(4) DENT, C and KROL A A (1987). Municipal Solid Waste Conversion to Energy: The Potential for Collaborative Research and Development between the UK, Sweden and Canada. Harwell Report (Available through HMSO).

UK

---

1. No nationally directed waste disposal policy. National government plays a non-interventionist but review role.

2. Waste Disposal Authorities and Energy Utilities have very separate statutory duties. Unco-ordinated approach to EFW (cf Sweden).

3. Landfill regarded as economically attractive and accepted practice. Over 90% of MSW is landfilled.

4. Only 5 major mass incineration plants with energy recovery. Little activity since local government re-organisation in 1974.

5. Substantial potential market for RDF. 4 operating plants manufacturing RDF pellets. However, general view that this route still not a sufficiently reliable alternative to landfill or even incineration.

SWEDEN

---

1. MSW seen very much as a _resource_ rather than a waste.

2. Environmental considerations have a very high profile, particularly the concern over emissions from MSW incineration (1985 moratorium, lifted 1986).

3. Landfill space is said to be limited.

4. Incineration linked to district heating is the major EFW route (50% of all MSW) and is regarded as economically favourable.

5. Future for all EFW routes looks promising (shortage of primary fuels, phasing out of nuclear power, philosophy of waste utilisation).

CANADA

---

1. Cheap energy (electricity and gas).

2. Regulatory climate different in each Province.

3. Landfills mostly too small or too remote for gas extraction and utilisation.

4. Most of EFW activity concentrated in Ontario. Public concern over emissions from MSW incinerators.

5. MSW incineration with energy recovery the only major EFW technology. 5 major MSW operating plants (others, including industrial/commercial waste incineration, under construction or consideration).

Table 1 Summary of the climate for energy from waste (EFW) technology
in the United Kingdom, Sweden and Canada

UNITED KINGDOM

1. Landfill Gas

o Substantial funding (Department of Energy and Department of the Environment).
o Includes research in following areas:
- laboratory studies, landfill gas optimisation;
- landfill microbiology and biochemistry;
- gas collection and extraction systems;
- major test cell programme;
- environmental impact.

2. RDF Production

o Substantial funding of research in recent years from DoE (Doncaster & Byker experiments).
o Important area highlighted for future research: selective pretreatment of MSW (and investigation of improvement in emission levels).
o Process plant modelling programme (US/UK bilateral agreement).

3. RDF Combustion

o Substantial funding.
o Two major programmes;
- RDF characterisation programme;
- RDF combustion trials.

4. Incineration

o Limited research funding.
o Emissions monitoring programme (but on much reduced scale to that of Sweden or Canada).
o Future research will probably concentrate on examination of benefits of MSW pretreatment and optimisation of combustion conditions (wrt emissions).

5. Other Thermal Processing

o Limited research (e.g. Manoil).

6. Demonstration Projects

o Financial support of selected EFW schemes to encourage wider adoption of the technology.
o Schemes include use of landfill gas, RDF and non-hazardous industrial/commercial wastes.

SWEDEN

1. Landfill Gas

o Expanding programme (broad source of funds directed through one agency).
o Field studies on the following topics:
- gas abstraction systems;
- operating problems (e.g. condensate, equipment)
- environmental impact;
- safety standards.

2. RDF Production

o Very little government sponsored R&D at present.
o Extensive operational study conducted at 15 existing plants during 1981-1985.

3. RDF Combustion

o Main emphasis of R&D.
o Government/industry funded development and operational studies on circulating fluidised beds
o Emissions studies.

4. Incineration

o Extensive operational study conducted at existing facilities in 1981-1985.
o Extensive environmental impact study in 1985-1986
o Main emphasis on emissions reduction. Studies on:
- optimising combustion conditions;
- flue gas treatment;
- thermodynamics and kinetics of reactions.

5. Other Thermal Processing

o Pilot scale studies on gasification in plasma arc and circulating fluidised bed systems.

6. Demonstration Projects

o Financial support of flue gas treatment, RDF combustion and landfill gas schemes.

CANADA

1. Landfill Gas

o Very limited research.

2/3. RDF

o Production of RDF has terminated at the Ontario Resource Recovery Centre, Toronto.
o "Prepared MSW" combustion trials to come under NITEP.

4. Incineration

o Major EFW research programme - NITEP, 5 key areas:
- environmental/health impacts;
- sampling and analytical methods;
- link between combustion conditions and emissions;
- incineration and pollution control technology assessment;
- regulatory controls.
o 3 generic incinerator designs chosen for testing:
- two-stage combustion;
- mass incineration (untreated MSW);
- prepared burning (incineration of partially treated MSW).
o Development of rotary kiln MSW incinerator; recent trials with aim of optimising emissions by internal modifications to kiln, lime addition and flue gas treatment.

5. Other Thermal Processing

o Feasibility study: gasification of MSW by Plasma Arc.
o Pyrolysis work (in particular, waste tyres but some MSW).

6. Demonstration Projects

o Federal and Provincial funding of a range of EFW projects.

Table 2   Summary of the research and development (R&D) on EFW technology in the United Kingdom, Sweden and Canada [1, 2, 3]

Substance	Flue Gas Emissions(1)		Total Swedish Emissions due to Incineration			
			Incineration of(2)(5) 1.4 M tonne per year		Incineration of(2)(6) 2.5 M tonne per year	
	Present situation	After(4) measures	Present situation	After(4) measures	Present situation	After(4) measures
Particulates	50	20*	420	170	750	300
Mercury, Hg	0.4	0.08 3)	3.3	0.7 3)	5.9	1.2 3)
Cadmiun, Cd	0.05	0.02	0.5	0.2	0.8	0.3
Nickel, Ni	0.002	0.001	0.02	0.01	0.04	0.02
Copper, Cu	0.2	0.06	1.5	0.5	2.7	0.9
Lead, Pb	3	0.5	25	4.0	45	7
Hydrogen chloride, HCl	1000	100*	8400	840	15000	1500
Hydrogen fluoride, HF	10	1	85	8	150	14
Sulphur oxides, SOx	400	200	3400	1700	6100	3000
Nitrogen oxides, NOx	400	400	3400	3400	6100	6100
Polyaromatic hydro-carbons, PAH	100	0.1	840	0.9	1500	1.6
Dioxins, TCDD equiv.	25	0.1-2.0**	225	9	400	10

1) Given in mg/Nm³, except for dioxins which are given in ng/Nm³ (both dry gas 10% CO_2).
2) Given in tonnes per year, except for dioxins, which are given in g per year.
3) Product control measures and collection of batteries should make it possible to reduce this value by 70-75%.
4) Utilising optimised combustion and advanced flue gas cleaning.
5) Current level of MSW incineration.
6) Most MSW and some industrial waste incinerated.

* calculated as a monthly average.
** 0.5-2.0 for existing incinerator
 0.1 for new incinerator

Table 3 Emissions from municipal solid waste (MSW) incinerators in Sweden

Process	Net Cost, £/tonne		
	UK	SWEDEN	CANADA
Landfill	1-7[1] (2.4-6.1) + (30-100)%[2]	5-10	2.3-7.3[9]
Landfill Gas Recovery/ Utilisation (additional costs to landfill)	-2.5[3]	-(0.7-10)[5]	NA
Mass Incineration	3-22[1]	3[6]	c 12.5 (steam production)[9] c 25 (electricity production)
RDF production and Sale	6[4]	22.9[7] 4.7[8]	NA

NOTES:

Negative values indicate a net profit.
NA   not available.
(1) CIPFA statistics (England and Wales only) 1986/7 estimates.
(2) Waste Management Paper No 26; range due to economies of scale, operating costs, plus percentage for capital and overhead costs.
(3) Approximate value used internally at the Environmental Safety Centre, Harwell.
(4) ETSU estimate.
(5) Net cost (real annuity method over 10 years) minus net income for current schemes.
(6) Incinerators with heat recovery, net average cost at Swedish 1983 prices.
(7) Net average cost, Swedish 1983 prices.
(8) Projected value if all produced RDF and compost were sold, Swedish 1983 prices.
(9) 1986 economic analysis for the Ontario Province.

See references (1)-(4) for more detailed discussions of these economic analyses.

Table 4 Net costs of disposal via the major EFW routes and landfill [4]
(1986 prices unless otherwise stated)

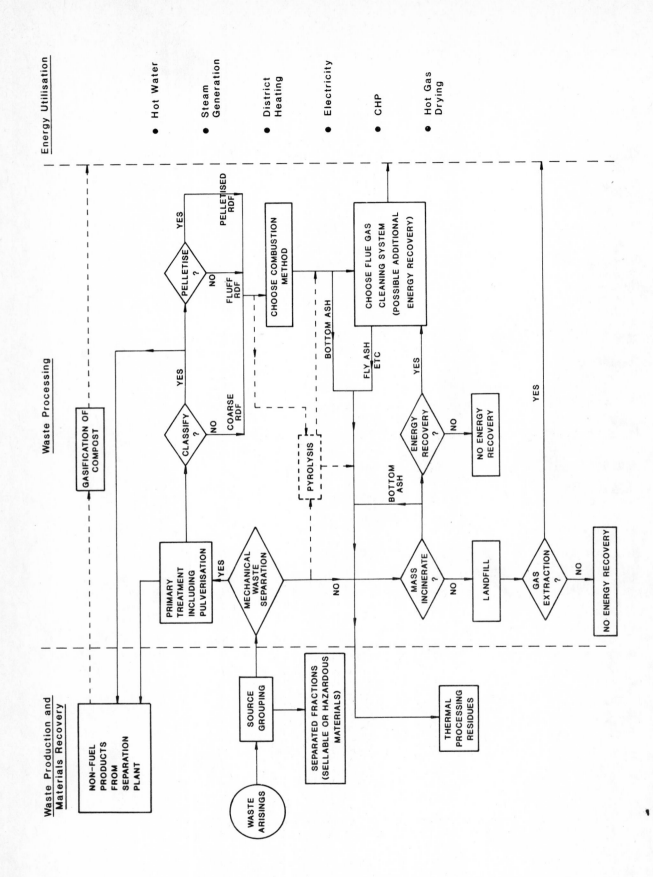

Fig 1   Decision framework for current uptake of EFW technology
         – – – – potential routes

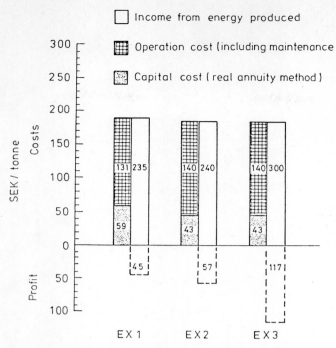

Fig 2   Economics of operating eight Swedish mass incinerators with sale
of heat to district heating, 1983 prices (10 SEK ≈ £1) [2]

Example I   Economic result with real income and real
utilisation time (62%), 1983.

Example II   Economic result with real income from 1983 but
with 100% utilisation time.

Example III   Economic result with all energy sold at a price
of 150 SEK/MWh and 100% utilisation time.

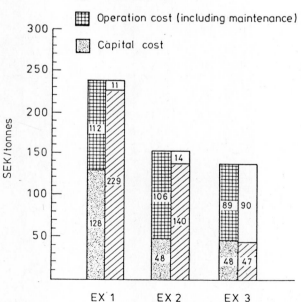

Fig 3   Economics of operating eight Swedish separation-composting plants
with sales of refuse derived fuel (RDF) and compost, 1983 prices
(10 SEK ≈ £1) [2]

Example I   Economic result with real income and real
utilisation time (44%), 1983.

Example II   Economic result with real income from 1983 but
with 100% utilisation time.

Example III   Economic result with all compost sold at a price
of 30 SEK/tonne and all RDF at a price of 150 SEK/
tonne, and with 100% utilisation time.

The unique W+E concept for enegy from waste

R SCHLEGEL, MSc
W + E Environmental Systems Limited, Zurich, Switzerland

SYNOPSIS   The W+E waste-to-energy plants are thermal power plants fired with municipal or industrial waste. This system, developed by W+E, consists of a feeding device, combustion system, combustion capacity control, and a boiler with mechanical cleaning device. The heart of this sophisticated combustion system is the W+E double motion overthrust grate which is arranged in a horizontal position. The boiler concept, also developed by W+E, allows high operational availability of the plant and a good flue gas burn-out. The energy obtained can be used for electricity, process steam or district heat.

1   INTRODUCTION

W+E Environmental Systems, Inc. is a Swiss based engineering and general contractor firm. W+E's business is to develop state-of-the art waste-to-energy technology to treat municipal waste and hazardous chemical waste and to build small as well as large scale incinerator plants all over the world, utilizing its own technology. W+E's proprietory technology for burning hazardous waste has become the premier technology for large scale plants in Europe.

In the seventies, W+E developed a unique concept to convert municipal waste into energy. This W+E concept consists of three main components:
- double motion overthrust grate
- tail-end boiler with mechanical rapping device
- integrated combustion control system
(figure 1)

The heart of the combustion system is the grate. The double motion overthrust grate has been specially designed for the combustion of municipal waste and similar products. The opposed motion of the grate bars creates a positive forward movement of the waste over the whole length of the grate.

The W+E resource recovery boiler comprises furnace, three radiation chambers and a horizontal convection section - the tail end - which includes superheater, evaporator and economizer.

It is obvious that continuous operation for up to 8000 hours in one year requires high tech controls. Only integrated combustion control systems make it possible for waste-to-energy plants to be operated like power plants. The overall control system also plays a crucial role in meeting environmental requirements. Only highly sophisticated combustion technology combined with an integrated control system can assure low emissions of CO, C_xH_y and dioxine.

2   WASTE FEEDING SYSTEM

Waste is admitted to the combustion system through a water-cooled feed chute which is lined with abrasion resistant steel plates. A hydraulically operated damper is provided to close the chute to eliminate air ingress, if required. The refuse falls by gravity onto a feeding platform from where two waste ram feeders, arranged one on top of the other (figure 2), will push the fuel onto the grate. Control of cycle times and stroke length permit the feed rate of the fuel to be varied in accordance to the waste composition, or as required by demand signals from the steam generators.

While designing this feeding system, our engineers paid special attention to operational reliability and easy maintenance.

3   COMBUSTION GRATE

As already mentioned, the heart of the combustion system is the W+E double motion overthrust grate. One of the main characteristics of this W+E grate, at a first observation, is its horizontal position (figure 3).

When this grate system was developed eight years ago, the following objectives were aimed at:

- high operational reliability

- good adaptability to changing waste composition

- environmentally relevant conditions (NO_x)

- easy maintenance

Seen in direction of material flow, the W+E double motion overthrust grate is constructed following a system of movable and fixed grate bars (figure 4). Looking at the grate from the side, we see that the movable bars work in opposed motion to the fixed bars between them.

A special bearing of the main driving shafts moving the flexible grate bars back and forth causes a translator movement of the bars. This system, when practically applied, is surprisingly simple; as mentioned above, the flexible grate bars move in a straight line and not in a circle. This motion process is of crucial importance to the obturation of the grate bar ends and the fixed grate bars lying below them. The driving shafts are driven individually by hydraulic cylinders; but there is also a possibility of actuating several grate bar rows together, depending on the fuel combusted on the grate. On the other hand, they could also be moved in pairs, in double motion or even running in the same direction. The grate is constructed in modules, of which each module represents an under-grate blast zone. The size and throughput capacity of the W+E grate is a function of the grate width (up to 33 bars in parallel) and the grate length (up to 5 zones). Beyond that, larger capacities are obtained by using two or even three grate sections in parallel; therefore we have a great flexibility in determining the grate width by simply joining several grate sections. We are able to manufacture combustion units in a modular design assembly technique from small to very high capacities, without having to work out new constructions. The maintenance of this system is very easy, since all movable parts are outside and easily accessible during operation even on grates with two or three sections. Through the horizontal position of the double motion overthrust grate, the waste or the waste mixture is automatically pushed forward. The double motion movement produces a good stoking effect and forms a kind of drop, which causes the already ignited waste to mix thoroughly with the non-ignited waste.

Even though the temperature ranges between 250 and 300°C only, the grate bars are made of high-alloy cast steel. Thus, damages caused by a temporary lack of air in a particular zone because of an operation error, can be avoided. This kind of arrangement is called an emergency running property of the grate.

The grate bars are not coated and are automatically cooled by the undergrate blast. Particular attention has been paid to the form of the air outlets, since these are of the utmost importance for the operational reliability. The individual grate bars are joined in a particular way, so that there is no need for pressure from outside the grate. Therefore, theoretically, grate sections of any width could be manufactured. If grate bars need to be exchanged, the coupling is easily released, and as a result it is not necessary to dismantle the whole grate lining. Seen from the side, each 2nd grate bar of the fixed and the movable system is moved in a relative shift in its end position. This system is very reliable and is mainly responsible for keeping the primary air outlets from choking. Therefore, cooling of the grate bars is always assured and the air distribution is kept at a constant level over the whole fuel bed. This even distribution over the whole grate is of crucial importance for the process of incineration, and because it reduces the forming of nitrogen monoxide or other toxic compounds. To a certain extent, the durability of the grate bars also depends on the cooling. It happens over and over again that a grate which is operated with insuffcient primary air, i.e. insufficient stoichiometric or even under stoichiometric conditions, suffers considerable damages so that the grate lining has to be exchanged after a very short time because of insufficient cooling and the interaction of oxidation / reduction. Not only the clean air outlets are important for a good air distribution, but also the pressure loss above the whole grate. As mentioned above, the way the grate bars are arranged and fixed creates a very tight grate surface. As a matter of fact, the primary air only gets into the fuel layer through the air outlets; hence not through any leakpoints in the grate lining. In addition, the amount of grate riddlings, which may also contain uncombusted or putrescible elements, is very small. It is approximately 0.2 - 0.5 kg per ton of waste.

Measurements made on a facility with an old and a new furnace have proven that the new grate system produces an average of 15% less thermal NOx. This is mainly the result of an even distribution of air over the whole grate and a uniform temperature field above the respective zones.

Because of its modular design the grate can be completely assembled, and the test run performed in the shop. A grate section can then, for example, be transported on a low-loader. The hydraulic station with its pumps is designed to operate the damper in the feed chute, the grate feeder, grate and ram discharger. Each pump can take the 100% load. The second one is the emergency pump and can be started immediately in case of failure.

While designing our system, we have also taken into consideration that no cooling plates on the sides of the grate would be necessary if we achieved a perfect combustion process on the grate. This was put into practice in Zurich-Hagenholz for the first time. Cooling plates normally protect the side walls from slagging. But in this case, uncontrolled air can get into the combustion chamber and impairs a good gas burn-out. Measurements performed on facilities with and without side plates show how far dioxine and furane are developed in these boundary zones. We could well imagine that the development of such toxic compounds takes place in these areas.

4   COMBUSTION CAPACITY CONTROL

When we developed our combustion system, we had a far-reaching automation in mind. The combustion capacity control shall not only relieve the operating personnel in their work, but also contribute to avoid undefinable conditions above the grate or in the combustion chamber at changing loads; it shall also help to control the combustion process in any situation. In our opinion, this is a vital measure to avoid any development of polyaromatics, and we have therefore paid special attention to it.

Although it is not possible to give a very broad account of the matter within the scope of this paper, it is worth mentioning that in our combustion capacity control the steam flow usually serves as input variable. As already mentioned, the grate feeder as well as the grate and the combustion air are controlled by a programmable control. But the combustion chamber temperature and the minimum O_2-content range above the other variables in consideration, since they are of vital importance for an optimal, controlled combustion. As a result, normal operation conditions can easily be re-established during control processes. For example: if at a required output change, the O_2-content will drop below the indicated O_2-threshold, the waste feeding is stopped immediately, and the O_2-content is re-established automatically. This control system makes it possible for us to incinerate relatively small layers of waste on the grate. Any uncontrolled burning of waste heaps caused because of lack of air or under very high temperatures can be avoided by burning only small layers of waste on the

grate. The control system, the optimal grate design and the possibility to incinerate small layers of waste are advantages that enable us to meet the set steam flow most easily. Consequently, a most constant steam production finally allows a constant generation of electric current and therefore, of course, brings about higher profits on the energy sold.

Figure 5 shows deviations of set values of different facilities. The % deviations mean that during 95% of the operating time, the actual energy production was within these deviations.

5   MEASURING VALUES

Figure 6 shows values of slag burn-out of the facilities Baden, Bielefeld, Øra (Frederikstad), Ingolstadt, Kisa, Schwandorf 1, 2 and 3, Uppsala I + IV and Zurich-Hagenholz.

6   BOILER SYSTEM

6.1 Furnace
   ———————

The typical W+E resource recovery boiler is comprised of a furnace, two radiation chambers and a horizontal convection section which includes superheater, evaporator and economizer.

The boiler was conceptually designed by W+E. The W+E configuration has developed over the years from vertical boilers with soot blowing to vertical boilers with shot cleaning, and finally to the present design featuring vertical tube bundles which are cleaned by mechanical rapping devices. Furnace walls are cleaned by pneumatic rappers.

The operating periods between major boiler cleanings have been improved by these design changes from 2000 to 3000 hours in early boilers to as much as 20,000 hours in modern boilers.

Concurrently with these design changes, the furnace volume was drastically increased and resulted in the 3-chamber arrangement which is generally utilized today for boilers operated with waste with a high heating value.

The following improvements are achieved by the increased furnace volume: The larger furnace volume results in significantly less slagging of the furnace walls, which in turn results in better boiler performance and increased operational availability. Also, the 3-chamber design increases the gas residence time up to the superheater so that sufficient time is available for flue gas borne fly ash particles to burn out prior to impacting on the superheater tubes. This reduces the ash deposits on the superheater tubes and the corrosion associated with such deposit layers. Also, the radiant heat transfer in the radiation chambers reduces the gas temperature to a value below the critical temperature, at which high temperature corrosion could occur in the superheater.

Most importantly though, the increased residence time assures the destruction of dioxins, furans and polyaromatics, which became a legal requirement in Europe.

The boiler is equipped with welded waterwalls in the furnace, the radiation chambers and the convection section side walls, except for the economizer section. Here the gas temperature is too low to justify the expense of waterwalls. The roof is also water cooled. The superheater consists of a final and initial superheater with a spray desuperheating station between the two sections. The final superheater is arranged in parallel flow with the gas, in order to reduce the tube temperatures for corrosion protection. All other surfaces are arranged in counter flow. In the direction of the gas flow, the superheater is followed by two evaporator bundles and a final economizer bundle and two initial economizer bundles.

6.2 Cleaning System

W+E boilers are designed for on-line cleaning. This is done by mechanical rapping of the vertical tubes of the convection sections and by pneumatical rapping of the welded furnace walls. To this end, the lower headers of the pendant tube sections are equipped with an impact shaft, which will be hit by a free falling hammer rotating on a motor driven shaft alongside the boiler walls. Multiple hammers are located on a single shaft impacting on sequential headers in a predetermined sequence. Acceleration of the headers and tubes up to about 100 g are achieved, which causes the deposits to slide off the tube in a similar fashion as is experienced with electrostatic precipitator rapping systems.

The frequency of the rapping cycles, a function of the fuel quality, is adjustable. On the furnace walls, pneumatic rapping devices are used because of the various required installation elevations. Here, pneumatically caused acceleration acts upon an impact plate which is welded to a number of waterwall tubes.

The cycle for the pneumatic rappers is also controllable as a function of furnace deposit build-up.

6.3 Air Supply

Primary combustion air to the grate/boiler is supplied for each boiler separately by a primary air fan for each boiler which takes suction from the tipping hall. This maintains the tipping hall/bunker under a slight negative pressure which serves as dust and odor control in these areas.

Primary air enters the combustion system via partitioned grate zones, as mentioned before. Normally, the primary air is preheated in the cooling channels of the grate bars. However an additional steam-heated air preheater is installed in the primary air duct to assist in predrying of very wet fuel with low heat content, or to preheat extremely cold ambient air.

The secondary combustion air is supplied to the furnace by a secondary air fan for each boiler. These fans take suction from the higher elevations inside the boiler building to assist in building ventilation. To assure even distribution, the air is admitted to the furnace via a large number of nozzles in the front and rear walls of the furnace. The air is injected into the combustion chamber at a very high velocity to assure complete turbulent mixing of volatiles emanating from the primary combustion process on the grate. This assures a complete burn-out of all combustibles prior to leaving the furnace and also assures that all environmental requirements regarding the destruction of certain pollutants are met. The FD-fan at the end of the process line is designed with a large performance allowance above the design excess air requirement to allow for changes in fuel composition.

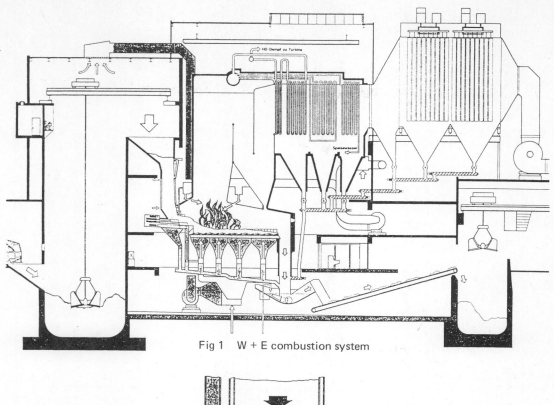

Fig 1   W + E combustion system

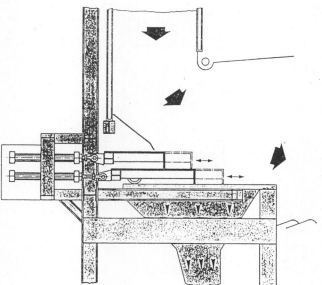

Fig 2   W + E double feeder

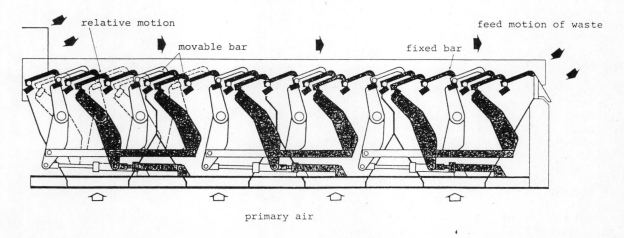

Fig 3   W + E double motion overthrust grate — longitudinal section

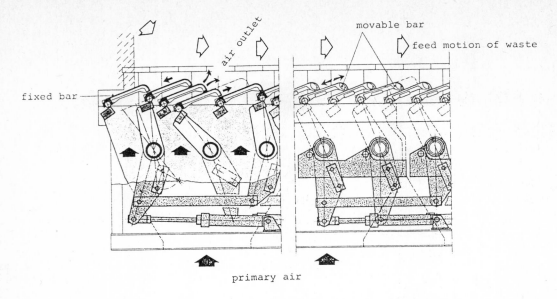

Fig 4   W + E double motion overthrust grate — function of the drive

	Steam △				
	Schwandorf 1,3	Uppsala 4	Zurich II	Baden-Brugg	Øra
95% of opera-ting time	± 5,5%	± 4,0%	± 6,7%	± 5,1%	± 3,4%

Fig 5   Set point deviation of steam

Plant	guaranteed %	measuring value %
Baden	5	3,6
Bielefeld raw/fine waste	5	1,7/2,3
Øra 1/2	3	2,2/1,8
Ingolstadt 3	5	1,0
Kisa	5	1,3
Schwandorf 1/2/3	5	2,4/1,8/1,9
Uppsala I/IV	5	1,7/2,7
Zurich II	3,6	2,8

Fig 6   Noncombusted annealing residue in the slag

C08/88

Incineration and heat recovery from solid, liquid and gaseous waste streams

J A J CLARK, BTech, MIChemE, MIGasE
Robert Jenkins Systems Limited, Rotherham

SYNOPSIS   Incineration of solid, liquid and gaseous waste streams is an area which is receiving considerable attention by industry in its attempts to reduce costs by recycling and reuse of rejected potential resources.   This paper reviews some of the possible routes open to recovery of energy and combustion of waste streams and materials.

1   INCINERATION AND HEAT RECOVERY FROM SOLID, LIQUID AND GASEOUS WASTE STREAMS

Waste arises from many manufacturing operations and those providing services to the consumer. The majority of businesses nowadays are highly conscious of resources including rejects and waste products.

Typical of this consciousness is for example, the disposal of waste paper or cardboard for recycling. A further example is the disposal of solvents for purification and re-use.

Whilst smaller sites often use contract waste disposal for solid and liquid waste streams, it is often the case for large sites that it is an ongoing cost to have removed from site something which can be re-used to generate heat and save cost of fuel purchase.

For clarity it is perhaps appropriate to deal with each waste type in turn and discuss the feasibility and merits of energy from waste schemes.

With any waste combustion plant it is imperative that air pollution legislation needs to be carefully studied to ensure the correct form of gas cleaning plant, if required, is selected.

Currently, air pollution legislation is enforced by the local Environmental Health Department for commercial and some industrial premises. For more specialised works, particularly the chemical and metal industry, these come under the auspices of the Clean Air Inspectorate.

Prior to embarking on detailed studies the level of emissions which are required should be determined, although with fume incinerators these may themselves be required to abate a source of pollution.

2   SOLID WASTES

On sites where waste in excess of 10 tons per week is generated and when there is a significant usage of heat there is an undisputed case for considering incineration of the waste and recovery of the heat produced. Below this level economics are questionable.

The savings are twofold:

- a saving in fuel costs due to generating steam from waste.

- a saving in waste disposal costs since now only a small quantity of ash is removed from site.

In practice it is usually found that for normal industrial wastes the savings are split in the ratio of 1 to 2, between waste disposal savings and energy savings.

When looking at the operation of an 'energy from waste' plant it is important not to become carried away with complexity and automation. A sense of realism is important for the job in hand.

On plants which handle up to 50 tons per week it is likely that some form of operator will be required to man the waste disposal operation. On most large sites an individual is usually dedicated to removal of waste to a central point, and operating a compactor or loading a skip.

Above this level it is possible to provide a relatively high degree of automation to shred, store, convey and load the waste.

All the necessary pretreatment, storage and conveying adds to plant capital costs, running and maintenance costs. It can also be a significant source of downtime when breakdowns occur, therefore careful thought should be given to these systems.

It must be realised though that with all systems, even those which include sophisticated handling and preparation systems, the waste must be charged into the system and inevitably this requires manual labour at some point.

Taking into account the above and other necesssities, such as environmental and safety considerations, the ideal energy from waste plant should meet the following:

- It should be simple to operate and not easily abused.

- A level of automation commensurate with scale of operations and site needs should be incorporated.

- The plant should meet air pollution legislation with the minimum, or no gas cleaning equipment.

- The plant should be safe to operate.

For actually burning solid wastes two combustion systems are worthy of mention, the selection depends on the waste forms and mixture.

For a relatively homogeneous waste which is shredded or prepared, it is possible to burn very effectively with excellent heat recovery in a mechanically stoker fixed system such as a HYGROTHERM K.W. solid fuel fired forced circulation heater, employing thermal oil or water as a heat conveying medium to the process or heating system - refer to figure 1.

A word of caution is appropriate here since this type of plant, whilst not requiring auxiliary fuel, is totally incapable of burning waste of varying calorific value, varying bulk density or waste which is unprepared or contains any significant plastic content.

There is however an excellent case for units such as this in areas like the furniture and wood industry, or others which produce innocuous waste streams without significant plastics.

Fig 1   Hygrotherm solid waste fired thermal oil heater

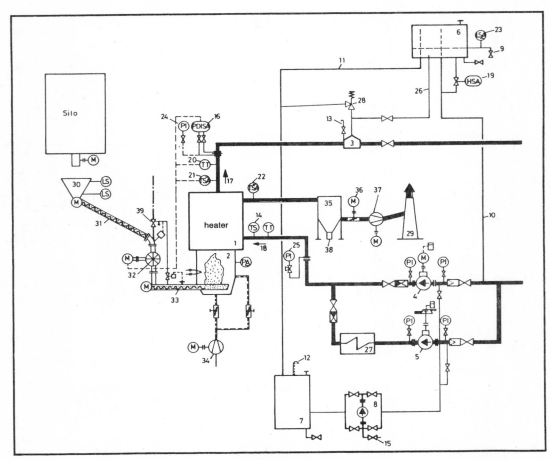

Hygrotherm System

1 Hygrotherm — heat-carrier heater	14 Flowmeter thermostat	27 Emergency cooler
2 Solid fuel firing	15 From barrel or tank truck	28 Safety valve
3 Separator	16 Flow safety device	29 Chimney
4 Centrifugal pump	17 Feed	30 Hopper
5 Emergency cooling pump	18 Return	31 Warm conveyor
6 Expansion tank	19 Quick-action stop device	32 Star feeder
7 Base tank	20 Feed-temperature control device	33 Stoker screw
8 Combined system filling equipment, manual or motorized operation	21 Safety temperature limiting device	34 Combustion air fan
9 Level monitoring device	22 Flue-gas temperature limiting device	35 Flue gas cleaner
10 Expansion line	23 Level limiting device	36 Low pressure regulating flap
11 Overflow and compensation line	24 Feed pressure gauge	37 Induced draught fan
12 Venting into open air	25 Return pressure gauge	38 Dust collection cask
13 Sample-taking point	26 Short-circuit line to expansion tank	39 Extinguisher

Wastes which contain high and varying levels of plastics are heterogeneous in form and problematical to shred, the most effective combustion plant is a starved or controlled air incinerator such as the CONSUMAT. It is probably not an exaggeration to state that 95 per cent of all the latest generation of incinerators in the Health Service use this principle of operation - refer to figure 2.

The flue gases produced by this incinerator type contain very low levels of grit and dust. It is possible to recover heat from the flue gases by using a conventional firetube type shell boiler.

This boiler is similar in its control functions and safety features to most steam and hot water boilers commonly found in industry.

One major difference between a fired boiler and an incinerator/waste heat boiler combination is that in a situation requiring shutdown of the boiler it is necessary to divert the heat input to atmosphere or 'dump' it rather than extinguish the burner on a conventional boiler. A suitable bypass system is therefore essential.

By this technique it is possible to continue the disposal of waste without the recovery of heat. This is of particular importance in the case of hospitals or research centres where an incineration facility is always required. A waste heat boiler, like any other boiler, requires an annual shutdown and inspection, the by pass also allows this to be undertaken.

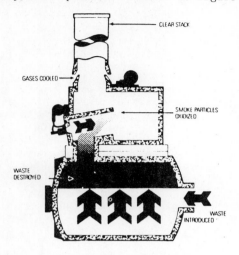

Fig 2   Basic design of Consumat starved air incinerator

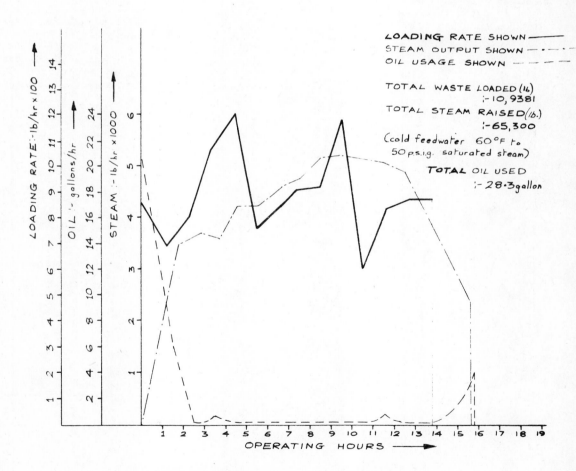

Fig 3   Performance of Consumat incinerator

In terms of overall performance and thermal efficiency it is important to realise that an incinerator and waste heat boiler is not as efficient as a normal fired boiler. This is so for numerous reasons, incineration is a process which often requires an excess of combustion air when compared to normal burners, additionally operating for one shift per day requires a significant amount of heat to bring the refractory and structure of the plant up to normal working temperature. The waste form, composition and moisture content also affect efficiency and recoverable heat.

Despite this the overall savings realised by the plant can still be worth the investment.

Figure 3 illustrates the energy output and auxiliary fuel usage of a plant operating in Southern Ireland which was commissioned in 1979 which has now operated for some eight years. The profile can be considered typical when burning a high calorific value of industrial waste such as that produced by a factory manufacturing carpets from polypropylene fibre.

The payback or justification for investment in a plant such as this depends on the relative purchase costs of energy for plant usage, waste disposal costs and capital cost. These vary considerably from site to site as do the methods of investment analysis used by companies. It is not within the scope of this paper to go into these costs in detail other than to say payback can be from 18 months upwards depending on site costs.

3 GASEOUS AND LIQUID WASTE STREAMS

The disposal of waste solvents, solvents or fume streams, presents in many cases a more attractive proposition than burning solid wastes. Many solvents are capable of being burned in properly designed equipment to produce hot water, steam or hot oil.

The essentials of the design of incinerators for these types of waste are largely governed by chemical equilibrium and thermodynamics and are classically related by the three "T's" of combustion.

Time :   Residence time at mean
                 incineration temperature.

Temperature :   Mean temperature to assure
                 adequate thermal oxidation of
                 the waste.

Turbulence :   Mixing of oxygen with the
                 organic waste.

Whether a fume or liquid waste is being incinerated, reactions take place in the gaseous phase. Liquids are elevated to their gaseous state by atomising into droplets followed by vapourisation of the droplets formed, in simple terms. The process is actually more complicated but this generalisation is sufficient for the aim of this paper.

A number of designs of fume and liquid incinerators, or thermal oxidisers, as they are also referred to, are on the market.

The HYGROTHERM unit illustrated in figure 4 is capable of burning fumes, aqueous liquids and organic liquids either singly or in combination.

The design of its burner and combustion chamber have been optimised to provide high turbulence levels in order to minimise potential dead or stagnant areas and a rapid approach time to the mean reaction or oxidation temperature. The result is a compact unit and the capability to burn a wide variety of effluent streams.

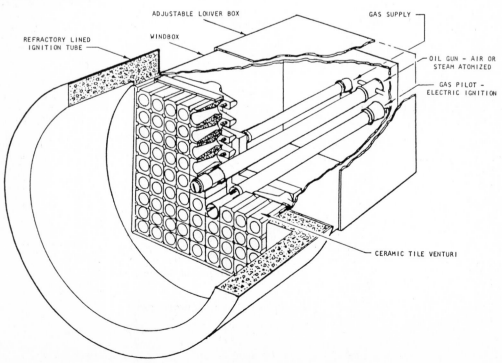

Fig 4   Hygrotherm liquid and fume burner

Typically these can be:

- organic fumes in air (diluted to 25% of lower explosive limit).

- organic fumes in inert carrier gases.

- neat organic waste streams.

- organic liquids.

- aqueous effluents containing organics.

As previously stated the advantage of the capability to burn multiple effluent streams is extremely useful since many sites have more than one effluent streams.

The use of waste heat recovery on these plants often has very short payback periods, sometimes a matter of months.

These systems also have more scope in the type of heat recovery, the following being normal methods of recovery.

Steam - generated at pressures up to 20 Bars.

Hot Water - generated at temperatures up to 150 °C.

Heat transfer oil - generated at temperatures up to 350 °C.

Air to air - this can be used either for fume preheating process or space heating.

Waste heat recovery is essential when incinerating low levels of organic vapours in air or odorous gas streams. Although systems exist which produce very high levels of heat exchange or recuperation of energy from incinerator off gases to preheat the fume passing into the incinerator these are inevitably expensive, very large and cumbersome and often use exotic alloys and maintain intensive forms of construction.

The installation of a fume incinerator with heat recovery should not be undertaken without a careful examination of all site energy requirements.

A typical heat balance for such a plant is shown in figure 5.

The extent to which heat may be recovered is dependent on the state in which it is required. The cost of a heat recovery plant in relation to the law of diminishing returns, and the temperature level to which stack gases may safely be taken. It may be possible to fit condensing economisers if natural gas is used for firing and the effluent stream forms non corrosive products of combustion.

In conclusion many combinations are possible - all need very careful assessment.

Appendix I

Referring to the CONSUMAT incinerator illustrated in Figure 3 the relative costs of operation and savings are summarised as follows:

- Capital cost of plant installed: £120000.00

Annual Operating Costs
- auxiliary fuel: £7500.00
- annual maintenance costs: £4400.00
Total: £11900.00

Annual Savings
- fuel saving in conventional boiler: £54800.00
- cost savings on previous waste
  disposal method: £14500.00
Total Savings: £69300.00
Nett annual saving: £57400.00

These costs were based on 1979/80 costs.

Electricity and labour costs are not included since no extra labour was required on site, also a similar quantity of electricity would be used in a normal boiler.

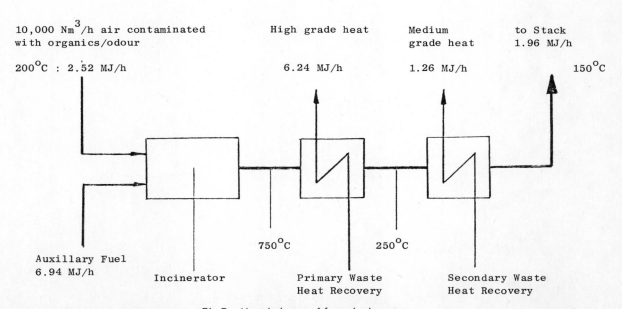

Fig 5   Heat balance of fume incinerator

Energy recovery from refuse incineration in the National Health Service

J W WALLINGTON, BSc(Eng), CEng, MIMechE
Welsh Office, Cardiff
R G KENSETT, BA, CEng, MIMechE, MCIBSE, MInstE, MBIM, FIHE
Welsh Health Common Services Authority, Cardiff

SYNOPSIS   In general, hospitals are committed to the incineration of the waste arising due to their day-to-day activities. This can be costly and as the waste products have a significant calorific value it makes sense to recover this heat energy provided that it is economic.

1.   INTRODUCTION

Hospitals produce considerable quantities of waste every day. The types of waste produced and the quantity varies according to hospital function.

Waste can be considered under two main categories:-
(a) In its 'domestic' form, ie clean newspapers, magazines, dead flowers, packing materials, etc
(b) That peculiar to the hospital, ie clinical waste in all its forms, which can be subdivided as follows:
   i. Pathological waste in liquid and solid form
   ii. Contaminated waste from isolation wards
   iii. Human tissue
   iv. Animal carcases from research laboratories, possibly highly contaminated.
   v. Home and hospital renal dialysis waste
   vi. Radiological waste which may be in the form of contaminated dressings, injection pellets and isotopes.

Although Local Authorities have a responsibility placed upon them to accept and dispose of domestic waste, frequently this responsibility is accepted only with reluctance. Even where it is accepted, this still leaves a considerable residue for which the hospital has to make its own disposal arrangements.

A detailed investigation has been made of the waste arising at a variety of hospitals (1). Fig 1 shows the weight of refuse produced per bed for various types of hospital. Table 1 gives an analysis of typical samples of hospital waste.

One point worthy of note is the comparatively high percentage of non combustibles - some 27%. Much of the material was found to be tins of various types principally from the kitchens. There is also quite a high proportion of other metals present.

This study has shown that for a typical District General Hospital the current rate of waste production is averaging 6.4 kg/bed/day (14.3 lbs). It has also been shown that the calorific value of hospital refuse averages 15 mj/kg (6460 Btu/lbs). [Nearly one half that of a good quality coal.]

2.   CONTEXT

All the other papers in this conference are devoted to municipal or industrial waste heat recovery. This is the only paper devoting itself to waste heat recovery in the National Health Service.

To put this into some sort of perspective the similarities and the differences are listed below:-
(a) The total scale is small - only equivalent to one line of the Edmonton municipal plant.
(b) Intermittent operation - almost always only a day shift in operation and the type of labour is not of the best.
(c) The nature of the materials handled ie (i) Radioactive wastes (ii) Dioxins.
(d) CV of hospital waste is better than municipal waste probably because of its high plastic content.
(e) NHS is committed to incineration so energy is available to save, but only if it is worthwhile as the NHS also has to operate broadly in accord with normal commercial criteria.

3.   ALTERNATIVE METHODS OF APPRAISAL

The following is quick review of possible alternatives to illustrate why incineration is considered the only viable method.

Maceration and discharge into the sea or a tidal river has been considered and was in fact tried in the Mersey area but it gives rise to a major pollution and environmental problem.

Compacting has been considered as a possible means of disposal using the blocks of refuse as landfill. Again this is a method which legislation would render unsuitable for clinical waste. Costs are also high.

Pulverisation has been investigated but costs and power are comparable with compacting and there is still the problem of final disposal.

As the above methods are not, in general, feasible solutions for a health authority, the only remaining answer is incineration.

A recent report commissioned by the Greater London Council (2) came out very strongly in favour of incineration at hospital level. It found that, without question, this method was the most efficient, safest, easiest and most environmentally acceptable. It also found that in the majority of cases it offered the cheapest solution.

4.   RECOVERABLE HEAT

Being committed to incineration and as refuse has a significant calorific value, a viable way of recovering some of this heat energy and using it to offset the capital and running costs of the facility is worth consideration by health authorities.

This paper deals mainly with the recovery of heat in separate waste heat boilers, but some other possibilities are direct combustion in admixture with other solid fuels (coal) or direct combustion of waste alone. (Section 8)

Waste incineration in hospitals is a priority in its own right so the incinerator design has to provide for the actual incineration process to be able to proceed whether or not the heat recovery equipment is in use. In practice by-pass facilities are invariably provided on the gas handling side of the installation.

As with all heat transfer applications, the heat theorectically available in the heat transfer medium is not necessarily the quantity of heat which will be economic to recover.

5.   HEAT GENERATION

When hospital waste is burned, it is wise to limit the temperature of the gas at the entry to a boiler to a maximum of about 1000°C (mainly due to the low temperatures at which entrained ash particles from the waste will fuse - between 975° and 1075°C). In practice, gas temperatures are commonly about 800°C due to the cyclic nature of waste feeding and to the need to minimise the use of a supplementary fuel. At these temperature levels, the excess air present at the exit from the secondary burning chamber is between 100 and 200% and the CO_2 in the gases varies from 5 - 10% (average about 7.8%). In these conditions, it is reasonable to assume that the heat released is either available in the hot gas or is lost (3).

It is necessary for some estimate of the calorific value to be taken and strictly the net calorific value should be used to be comparable with other boiler plant. In the authors' experience, a suitable value for the gross calorific value of general hospital waste is 17.4 mj/kg (7500 Btu/lb) - adjusted upwards if necessary to accommodate exceptionally high proportions of plastic.

Auxiliary fuel can be allowed for from the burner setting data and a heat balance can be performed in the manner shown in Appendix A.

6.   HEAT RECOVERED

6.1.   Maximum Possible Recovery

This assumes that the exit gas temperatures from the boiler is taken down to the lowest prudent level - usually 200-230°C.

Design is then based on the following assumptions:-

(a)   The calorific value is accurately known.
(b)   The gas design temperature selected is accurate and thus the mass of flue gas calculated is also accurate.
(c)   The heat loss assumed is accurate (usually 5%)
(d)   Feeding of the incinerator is continuous.

Calculations indicate that 70% of the heat input to the incinerator can be recovered. Only about 65% is ever obtained in practice.

6.2   Partial Heat Recovery

In this case a deliberate choice is made for less than the maximum recovery. The reasons for such a choice might include:

(a)   heat recovery for a limited purpose;
(b)   insufficient heat load.

7.   ADDITIONAL CAPITAL COSTS

7.1   Gas by-pass and Additional Gas Handling Plant

The facility for gas by-passing is essential in hospitals which have a single incinerator to preserve the incineration function. This requires air cooling of the flue gases to about 400°C and a chimney working on natural draught. Where the chimney can be directly mounted on the incinerator this is relatively simple. There is a big difference in the cooled volume of incinerator gases (originally at 800°C say) at the exit of a boiler and that of the same volume cooled to 400°C by air dilution. The ratio of volumes is about 2.75:1. As a result the same chimney size is required as for non-waste heat recovery working.

Except on the very simplest systems, it is necessary to use an induced draught fan to over come the draught loss in the boiler and to preserve an underpressure in the incinerator.

7.2 Mechanical and Electrical Services

The connection of the heat recovery plant into the main hospital heat distribution system may require a substantial amount of pipework and pumping equipment. With the boiler house adjacent this cost is usually significant, but with a remote incinerator house it can be sufficient to render a scheme uneconomic.

7.3 Additional Building Costs

Although waste heat boilers can be designed for outside installation at modest cost, the majority of installations have the boiler installed in a purpose built house. This cost must be considered.

7.4 Instrumentation

Additional instrumentation must be provided to measure the quantities of steam or hot water raised. The flow of auxiliary fuel must also be monitored and it is extremely useful to have a means of assessing the quantities of waste incinerated.

8. OTHER TYPES OF INCINERATION

8.1 Direct Waste Burning Boilers

The original concept of direct burning boilers is not new and in the period 1930-1960 many were installed in European and Scandinavian hospitals - proving suitable for the waste composition of those days, even when fired only with hospital waste. It was a small step to fit burners to aid solid residue burnout and smoke burning, but there were limitations on performance regarding smoke, gas composition and ash quality. There was also an unacceptable operator involvement and risk in cleaning fire-grates with working furnaces. Such furnaces performed poorly when plastic materials began to appear in waste, and concern grew for the quenching of combustion on water-cooled surfaces, especially some of the toxic and pathogenic species, and antineoplastic agents.

The supply of air for combustion was not controlled and the quality of performance depended totally on the ability (and patience) of the operator.

This type of equipment is intended to perform as a boiler and as an incinerator simultaneously and separately. There are two main types of furnace:

(a) Co-firing with coal.
(b) Co-firing with gas or oil fuel.

The major difference is that with coal there is a solids emission from the coal as well as from the waste. Similarly there is also a solid residue from the coal firing.

This method of waste disposal is still being evaluated but the waste heat recovery from combined burning looks very attractive.

The heat exchange equipment does not have to be duplicated (assuming that any capital costs for the waste handling and shredding equipment can be equated to those for conventional incinerator purchase).

The burning capacity which can be made available depends on:

(a) Ratio of coal to waste (typically 2:1)
(b) Normal coal consumption of the boiler.

Thus, a boiler burning say 500 kg/hour of coal will be able to burn about 250 kg/hour of shredded waste. However, if the boiler equipped for waste burning has to be turned down during periods of low heat demand, the rate of waste burning will be reduced also - needing an extended period of burning. This factor would appear to be critical in sizing of plant. There is no published information yet on how such plants perform.

8.2 Low Energy Incinerators (zero fuel)

This type of incinerator has been developed in reponse to repeated demands to reduce the usage of energy and it has been called the "fill and forget" incinerator. The basis for this type of combustion system is that of underfire combustion in which the fire progresses downwards from the top - thus feeding new waste effectively into the underside of the fire. Waste is fed into the incinerator in BULK quantities sufficient for several hours burning and there is a major saving in labour attendance. Apart from electrical ignition, no fuel energy is needed for incineration and operating costs are as low as a few pence per hour for electricity.

9. CONVERSION OF CONVENTIONAL BOILERS

It has proved feasible to modify installed boilers both steam and water. There often exists spare capacity in hospital boilerhouses which cannot be used. Where there is a suitable layout of plant and where the size of boiler is also suitable this type of conversion can be very cost-effective. There are the natural advantages that all the services and pipework, etc are already installed and the total capital cost of such a conversion is not much more than the basic incinerator installation.

One main design criterion which must be met is that the total mass of gas from the incinerator must be near enough that mass of gas for which the boiler was designed on conventional fuel. In this way the tube sizes and heat exchange areas will be quite close to those which would be chosen for a purpose-designed waste heat boiler. Owing to the excess-air levels at which incinerators operate (at the exit of the secondary combustion chamber) a rule of thumb guide to the suitability of an existing boiler is that for the same mass of gas from the conventional burner and from incinerator, the recovered heat will be about half that on conventional firing. For example, if the heat in the incinerator gases is sufficient for 1500 kg/hour steam, then a conventional boiler sized for 3000 kg/hour will be adequate.

10. COST BENEFIT ANALYSIS FOR WASTE HEAT RECOVERY

As in all cases of energy efficiency or conservation there is no point in saving energy if the capital required to be invested to achieve this saving is so large that the financial equivalent of the energy saving will never repay that capital.

Those projects which have a simple payback time of less than three years will almost certainly be viable (ie Capital Cost ÷ Annual financial saving). This is a crude assessment and to evaluate more exactly the Net Present Value (NPV), Equivalent Annual Charge (EAC) or Internal Rate of Return (IRR) techniques must be employed. [5]

As a result of the many variations which come about when a technically correct installation is made, it is necessary to assess each case fully and individually to identify when the financial returns in a particular set of circumstances may be insufficient. Also, there are different levels to which an installation needs to be equipped and instrumented - mainly according to the working pressure of the heating system. It is not possible to arrive at an estimate of recovered heat unless careful account is taken of the effect of operational disciplines, for the way in which a facility is managed can make a greater difference to the recovery. It is better to have a lower output heat recovery unit which can be kept fully utilised than a larger one (more capital!) which is only partly effective.

11. WORKING SYSTEMS FOR WASTE HEAT RECOVERY

There are now a number of waste heat recovery systems in operation within the Health Service in association with incinerators. At October 1987 the totals were as follows:

Plants in operation	82
In planning/under construction	18
	100

12 THE FUTURE

In the burning of waste, there are several environmental criteria to be satisfied to provide fully acceptable control of the solid and gaseous effluents from the process. In the development of legislation on environmental matters, incinerators have not yet been covered as completely as certain other combustion equipment, and for many years now presumptive standards have been adopted for new plant installations. It is expected that standards will be developed as the need arises, mainly as quantitative emission requirements are incorporated into pollution legislation [6]

Environmental Health Officers (EHOs) appear in the past to have been rather generous in their approach to the operation of these facilities - many incinerators discharge their combustion products through very short chimneys. Compare this with the very stringent requirements imposed on exhaust chimneys from boiler plants. There has also been some concern expressed about the discharge of PCBs and radioactive substances.[7] Incineration of PCBs is the subject of continuing research and the residual radioactivity of incinerated isotopes is usually at a level low enough to cause no concern.

All this has led to the perception that health service incineration needs to be brought gradually under a tighter control both from the installation standpoint and from that of plant operation.

The Conference will no doubt be aware of the proposals contained in the recent Consultative Paper. [8]

Comments have been invited from interested bodies including the Engineering Institutions.

The proposals may be summarised as follows:

(a) To retain the principles of control through the use of "best practicable means" adapted to take account of existing and proposed EEC Legislation.
(b) To give Local Authorities powers of control including prior approval over certain processes.
(c) To provide a system of 'consents' accessible to the Public which will set out the main elements of 'best practicable means' agreed for the installation by the control authority.
(d) To improve Public access to information about air pollution control.

As part of the proposals NHS incinerators would be a scheduled process where it would be an offence to operate without following the 'consents' procedures. When these proposals are considered in conjunction with the removal of Crown Immunity (which does not and never did imply a poorer system of operation and control) the NHS may well need to reconsider its position as regards on site incineration. The more rigorous control will include boilers adapted to burn waste or waste derived products as the secondary fuel.

The scheduling will place both incinerator installers, the Regional Health Authorities and the operators, the District Health Authorities, under a statutory obligation to meet the required terms of the Best Practicable Means Agreement. The extent to which this duty was carried out would require to be publically demonstrated by both the terms of consent and subsequent monitoring of results.

'Best Practicable Means' are not clearly defined and, unless this is done it could lead to confusion. When one realises that one Environmental Health Officer suggested that this would mean a gas washer on an incinerator operating 4 hours per day and burning some 80 kgs/hour, the likely problems will be appreciated.

In consequence, discussions are already in progress as regards possible centralisation of incineration on a District basis, siting the plant both centrally and in a designated industrial area.

Whilst there may be problems as regards transporting the waste, it would mean the installation of large plants with approved 'best practicable means' of limiting emissions of both particulate and chemical matter. Such means would be both practical and economic on the larger plants which they could never be on smaller individual hospital incinerators.

This being the case there would be obvious and much increased advantages in applying heat recovery to the installation. In the case of centralisation for one of the larger Districts the loading would be in the order of 75 000 lbs per day (32 000 kg/day) which, in the higher CVs of hospital waste could offer the potential of recovering some 500 000 Mj. Not large by municipal standards but none the less well worthwhile.

13. CONCLUSIONS

There is a good potential for energy recovery from burning hospital waste and a number of installations have been in operation for some time. There are a wide range of possible implementations each of which have their own particular requirements.

The successful installations of waste heat boilers in hospitals need the application of reasonable management discipline to maintain the tempo of operations and of maintenance. Both the arrival of waste at the incinerator and the loading of that waste in a practical rhythm are essential to success, for the consumption of fuel in unattended operator periods is punishing as regards economy.

Additionally, incinerators differ from fired boilers in one important aspect, namely that the incinerator air supply is usually fixed and the waste must be provided as necessary. Consequently, if waste supplies are uneven, air which enters the incinerator is unused by combustion and passes to the boiler too cool to give useful recovery of heat - such losses can be serious. The performance varies also according to whether all of the combustion products from burning of waste are passing to the boiler or are partly by-passed for reasons of heat load or design of the system.

Each case must be considered individually on its own merits and a formal investment appraisal carried out. Detailed case studies are given in the Appendices.

REFERENCES

(1) DHSS - 'Disposal of Hospital Waste'. Hospital Service Engineering Data Sheet MW 2.1 - 2.39 August 1973.

(2) GLC - Working Party on Disposal of Clinical Wastes in the London Area - Final Report April 1983.

(3) CHAMBERLAIN, C T Energy Recovery from the Burning of Hospital Waste. 39th Annual Conference of the Institute of Hospital Engineering. Manchester 1983.

(4) DHSS/Welsh Office - ENCODE 2.

(5) HM Treasury - Investment Appraisal in the Public Sector - 1982.

(6) Department of Environment/Welsh Office - Consultative document "Air Pollution Control in Great Britain - Review and Proposals". December 1986.

(7) McCullough, John Letter to 'Chartered Mechanical Engineer' June 1987 p10.

(8) Idem 6

APPENDIX A

HEAT RECOVERY FROM INCINERATION

Consider a typical district general hospital of 800 beds

Refuse produced = 800 x 6.48 kg(from fig 1)

Assuming the incineratable waste to be 72% of total produced

Incineratable waste = $\frac{72}{100}$ x 800 x 6.48

= 3732 kg per day

A refuse load of this magnitude would probably be met by two incinerators each of capacity 600 lbs/hour (273 kg/hr).

∴ Daily load = 1866 kg per incinerator

and daily use = $\frac{1866}{273}$ = 6.8 hours*

Theoretical amount of heat released from refuse = 1866 x 15

= 27 990Mj(per incinerator)

Assuming a realistic recovery of 60% of the available heat released then

Heat recovered = 0.6 x 27 990Mj
= 16 794Mj

*Designed use 30hrs/week ie 6hrs/day but operation sometimes occurs for up to 11hrs/day.

To find the heat also given up by the auxiliary fuel, the consumption of 35 sec oil on average is 36.3 litres per hour for 6.8 hours

thus daily use of oil $= 36.3 \times 8$
$= 290$ litres

net CV of oil $= 38Mj/litre \ (45.6Mj/Kg)$

$\therefore$ Heat released from oil $= 290 \times 38$

$= 11 \ 040Mj$

If 60% of this is also recovered

Heat recovered from oil $= 0.6 \times 11 \ 040$

$= \underline{6624Mj}$

Thus total heat recovery $= 23 \ 418Mj$(per incinerator)

This is equivalent to 10 000kg of steam at 120psig (8 bar) (a normal pressure for use in hospitals).

Approximate value of this is £100 per day (per incinerator). This is equivalent to a total annual saving of £50 000 (for the two incinerators).

APPENDIX B

OUTLINE INVESTMENT APPRAISAL

Considering the installation in Appendix A, ie 2 x 600lbs/hr incinerators supplying a waste heat boiler which supplies an average of 3000kg/hr of steam into the main hospital distribution system at 120psig (8 bar).

Total capital cost of such an installation (including the element for waste heat recovery)

$= £142 \ 000$

But as noted in the body of the paper the basic cost of the incinerator can be considered as an essential requirement in terms of the normal operation of the hospital. Thus the capital investment to be considered for the purpose of appraisal is the extra over cost for the waste heat recovery equipment including all necessary ducting, piping, fans, etc.

Additional cost for waste heat recovery $= £71 \ 000$

Revenue (recurring costs)

Oil $= £25 \ 6000$ per annum

Attendance by operators $= £0$ (as these operators will be required anyway and the waste heat boiler is virtually automatic)

Electricity (for induced draught fan) approximately 24kwh per day $= £300$ per annum

Thus using a test discount rate of 5% and assuming the incinerator has a useful life of 15 years

Equivalent annual charge of the capital investment $= \dfrac{£ \ 71 \ 000}{10.384*}$

$= £ \ 6 \ 837$ per annum

Annual cost of oil $= £25 \ 600$ per annum

Annual charge of electricity $= £ \ \ \ 300$ per annum

Total annual costs of waste heat recovery $= £32 \ 737$

Annual saving $= £50 \ 000$

Thus the hospital benefits to the tune of about £17 000 per annum

* from NPV Tables – Ref 5.

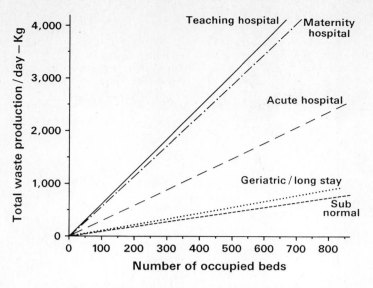

Combustible waste approximately 72% of total

Fig 1   Relationship between hospital function and waste production

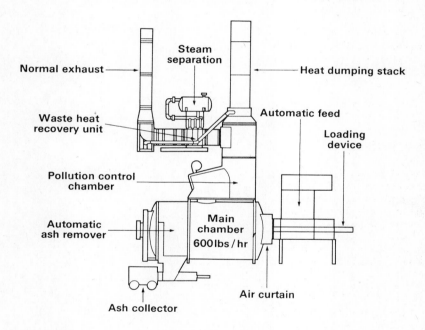

Fig 2   Typical modern waste heat/incineration installation for a hospital

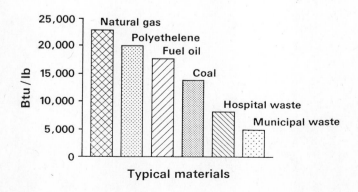

Fig 3   Comparative heating values

Constituent	per cent present	per cent corrected for non combustibles	CV for material Btu / lb Mean	CV equivalent Mj / Kg Mean
Paper — clean	9·55	13·2	7,400	2·27
— dirty	6·51	9·0	7,400	1·55
Ward and pathology waste	19·75	26·1	6,500	3·85
Kitchen waste	22·60	31·3	3,000	2·19
Non combustible waste	27·97	–	–	–
Plastics	14·62	20·4	8,500	4·05
Totals	100·00	100·0	–	13·91

Table 1   Typical constituents and calorific values of hospital waste

	Municipal	Hospital
	%	%
Paper	34	16
Kitchen waste	24	22
Plastic	5	14
Ward	–	20
Non combustible	37	28
	100	100

Table 2   The heating values of various types of waste

The combustion of waste in fluidized bed boilers — two case histories

F ELLIS and **C ARMITAGE**
Foster Wheeler Power Products Limited, Leeds
J O'NEIL and **D HOBSON**
Woolcombers Limited, Bradford, Yorkshire
R SHIPLEY and **D GOODWIN**
Robinson and Sons, Chesterfield, Derbyshire

SYNOPSIS   Two fluidised bed boilers supplied by Foster Wheeler to Industrial Users have successfully burned waste fuels.   This paper describes the waste fuels and the development of the combustion systems by the boiler owners, Woolcombers Ltd., Bradford and Robinsons of Chesterfield.   The two wastes have different properties and the problems encountered in handling and burning them are reported.   The first stage of development has been completed and savings due to reductions in primary fuel and disposal costs have been identified.

INTRODUCTION

Foster Wheeler Power Products Ltd. is a major contractor of boiler plant to the industrial and utility markets. The company supplies equipment to burn the complete range of liquid, gaseous and solid fuels. This paper describes the design and operation of two smaller industrial atmospheric fluidised bed boilers in which systems have been developed for the combustion of in-house wastes.

The boilers which were developed in collaboration with the N.C.B. (British Coal) are of the watertube design producing steam for space heating and process use.

Rising fuel prices have led to the increasing attraction of waste fuels, and several methods are available for the combustion of such materials. Both Woolcombers Ltd. and Robinson and Son's favoured fluidised bed technology as it was suited to burn coal products. Fuel costs at the time of project assessment justified the installation of the boiler plant, burning coal alone. Further savings have been demonstrated from the combustion of waste material.

The waste combustion systems have been developed by the respective companies. Both preferred to install a system and then develop it from "hands on" experience gained by actual operation of the equipment in a commercial environment. The alternative was to undertake a programme of design and pilot trials before exposing the development in the operating boiler plant.

Woolcombers Ltd., part of the Illingworth Morris Group, Bradford burn a highly fouling, high water content woolgrease. The heavy fouling problem has been overcome and the low calorific value effluent burnt, providing an alternative disposal method. The combustion system is in its final stage of development.

Robinson and Son's Chesterfield burn a bulky cellulosic material. Handling of the waste is labour intensive but it burns easily and cleanly within the boiler.

Both projects were sponsored by the Energy Efficiency Office of the Department of Energy through the Energy Efficiency Demonstration Scheme.

These brief case histories highlight the flexibility of fluidised bed technology to burn waste fuels, with diverse properties, substituting a portion of the primary fuel input.

BOILER DESIGN

The main operating parameters of the two boilers are given in table 1. The boilers are from a standard range of designs for coal firing. No special features were necessary in either unit to enable waste to be burned.

The design of the 10.2 MW (30,000 lb/hr) unit at Robinson and Son's is described in figure 1.

The boiler was constructed in three modules, comprising a generating bank with single drum and two fluidised bed modules. The design of the 7.1 MW unit at Woolcombers is similar to that of the 10.2 MW unit, however only a single fluidised bed module is required.

The fluidised bed design, licenced from British Coal is the atmospheric, shallow bed technology. The beds are nominally sized 2.0m x 2.5m. The distributor is constructed from watercooled surface, which forms an integral part of the boiler circulating system.

Standpipes on the fins between the tubes, forming the floor, distribute the fluidising air. The bed material consists of sized silica sand, at a static bed height of nominally 200 – 250mm. An inclined tube bank is positioned within the furnace, such that it is almost fully immersed in the fluidised bed at the maximum fluidising velocity. As the velocity is lowered, the amount of bed expansion reduces, and the tube bank is progressively uncovered. The bank is selected such that, at maximum output the bed temperature is 950 deg C. and the excess air level is 30%. A turndown of 2:1 per bed is possible and thus the larger boiler is capable of a 4:1 turndown by slumping one bed. Coal is delivered from bunkers by gravity through the furnace sidewalls. The coal presently burned at both sites is a washed singles.

The generating bank is of a straight tube construction between upper and lower headers. Horizontal baffles form multiple passes through the bank before the gas exits to an economiser and subsequent gas clean up equipment.

The boilers are operated under a balanced draught, resulting in a slightly negative furnace pressure. Start up is achieved by preheating the air at the inlet to the plenum using natural gas or diesel oil burners. Coal feed to the bed is gradually increased until normal bed operating temperatures are reached, and the burners are switched off. Fully automatic start up and load following is provided by the use of a solid state programmable logic controller. Load following is based on a step change philosophy in which the coal to air ratio remains fixed.

The Woolcombers 7.1MW unit was commissioned in 1982 and has since operated for over 30,000 hours.

Commissioning of the Robinson and Sons unit was completed in January 1985 and it has since operated for over 13,000 hours.

CASE HISTORY 1
WOOLCOMBERS LTD.

Woolcombers Ltd. is a wool processing company in Bradford, West Yorkshire. Energy consumption accounts for approximately 10% of the company's production costs and in 1982 Woolcombers installed a fluidised bed boiler as a means of reducing these costs. The fluidised bed boiler was selected because of its ability to burn both coal and a waste effluent produced in the wool scouring process. The company is subject to trade effluent charges for the disposal of the waste, a woolgrease with a positive calorific value.

Woolcombers produce a wool top which is the material from which Spinners produce yarn. In the production of top the raw wool is scoured in five bowl sets using hot water as the cleaning medium. The effluent from each of the stages is principly water contaminated with grease, sand and vegetable matter. The concentration of contaminants reduces in the effluent from each of the five stages.

Woolcombers originally discharged all of the effluent to drain, a service for which they are charged. They now concentrate the liquor from the first bowl. Figure 2 is a diagrammatic representation of the process. The effluent is initially settled and centrifuged to remove sand and lanolin, leaving a solution containing up to 94% water. This solution is stored and pumped on a continuous basis through a shell and tube heat exchanger before entering a two stage flash tank. The system is energy efficient utilising steam from the boiler, and returning the condensate to the hotwell. Low pressure steam produced from the flash tanks is used for space heating. A back pressure of 3 bar g is maintained on the system.

Problems have been encountered with the heat exchanger. Initially, the liquor passed through the shellside and the steam through the tubes. A substantial short fall in performance occurred owing to fouling of the outside of the tube surface. The exchanger was redesigned and a new tube bundle installed with the liquor passing through the tubes and the steam through the shell. The increased effluent velocity now maintains the surface in a clean condition.

Rapid erosion of the heat exchanger and associated pipework occurs owing to the abrasive action of sand in the effluent. Although settled and centrifuged, fine particles remain in suspension and frequent maintenance is required to keep the plant operational. Long term maintenance requirements are still being evaluated.

The resultant liquor has been concentrated to around 64% water. This reduction in volume allows it to be disposed of at a reduced cost, or alternatively to be burned in the boiler.

An analysis of the woolgrease is given in table 2. It was anticipated that, on combustion, fouling of heating surfaces would be a problem, owing to the high proportion of the alkali metals, particularly sodium and potassium. The net calorific value is low, due to the large percentage of ash and also, particularly, water. However trials performed at the outset of the project confirmed that the waste could be successfully burned.

Woolcombers Ltd. have developed a combustion system, principly by carrying out full scale trials in the operating plant. Initially the liquor was pumped directly, without atomisation, through a single nozzle located at a position just above the active area of the fluidised bed. (see figure 3, position A). Some of the material burned with a flame that carried into the furnace exit screen tubes and after 2-3 hours severe fouling had occurred. The remaining liquor poured into the bed and within 24 hours the bed had defluidised owing to clinkering from local overheating and/or fouling. At this time, there was no bed management system operational to allow on-line cleaning/regrading of the bed material.

© IMechE 1988 C12/88

Foster Wheeler Power Products carried out a series of deposition tests, firing coal and woolgrease with and without additives in their test facility at Hartlepool. The tests identified that combustion was improved by introducing the woolgrease in a fine spray and with air injection. There was indication that the use of the magnesium based antifoulant had some beneficial effect on the deposits, producing a lighter formation.

Woolcombers Ltd. designed a nozzle and introduced it into the freeboard of the boiler furnace. The nozzle incorporated primary and secondary air. Higher air pressures were found to result in better atomisation and combustion, however they also resulted in longer flame lengths. Trials were performed with the primary and secondary air until optimum settings were found suitable for the boiler width. Additives were also mixed with the woolgrease and although fouling of the furnace exit screen tubes still occurred, the deposits were soft, friable and easily removed. A steam lance, introduced through the furnace sidewall, removed most of the deposits from the screen tubes.

Finally the burner was repositioned in the expanded bed zone. (see figure 3, position B) Two nozzles were installed in the front corners of the furnace, directed diagonally to maximise flame length. Trials were performed to optimise air injection and nozzle diameter. A minimum hole diameter of 4.7mm was established to avoid blockage.

The arrangement was most successful and 225 litres per hour of woolgrease has now been burned on a regular basis for more than 4000 hours. Up to 450 litres per hour has been burnt over short periods of time without any detrimental effect to the boiler. A bed management system is now operational and fouling and defluidisation of the bed rarely occurs.

The woolgrease rate is controlled manually and separately from the boiler automatic control. The system is operated by the regular boiler operator. Proposed future development will integrate the waste firing into the boiler control system allowing unsupervised operation.

Furnace exit gas temperatures increase by up to 30 deg C. Boiler exit gas temperature increased by up to 20 deg C. within the first few hours of firing woolgrease. The temperature settles and only returns to it's normal level after approximately 24 hours of operation without woolgrease firing. The increase in temperature is attributed to fouling of the boiler surfaces from the woolgrease. This fouling has been noted during boiler inspections. The deposits are very light and it is considered that they are gradually removed during operation without woolgrease, allowing the gas exit temperatures to revert to their original, lower values.

Trials have been performed to prove the effectiveness of additives and to assess boiler performance. Primary fuel savings have been shown regularly when burning woolgrease. Table 3 illustrates a typical operating period, during which a primary fuel saving of 9.3% was recorded.

The cost of replacing the original evaporator unit and the, as yet, unevaluated maintenance and operating costs do not allow the meaningful calculation of a payback period for the project. However, if the system can be developed to dispose of the total liquor produced, the savings from disposal costs and the reduction in primary fuel will be in excess of .100,000/p.a. The resultant payback period for the heat exchanger and associated equipment would then be less than 12 months. A detailed economic assessment is soon to be published as part of the Energy Efficiency Demonstration Scheme.

Current Status

The two nozzle, air atomised system is installed in the front corners of the furnace, located just above bed height.

As much as 20,000 litre of Woolgrease have been successfully burned in a week at a maximum continuous rate of 225 1/h. Problems are still encountered with fouling of tube surfaces and very occasionally with solidification of the bed. The evaporator unit now requires repairing every three/four months and complete replacement will soon be necessary.

CASE HISTORY 2
ROBINSON AND SONS

Robinson and Son's, one of Britains largest privately owned manufacturing companies, mainly produces cotton wool and pulp cellulose products such as nappies.

Originally, steam was raised by gas fired shell boilers, however as with Woolcombers Ltd., energy costs instigated a change in fuel to coal. The ability to burn the large quantities of waste, produced in-house, favoured a fluidised bed. The steam produced is used in the manufacturing process and for space heating. The boiler is designed for the future addition of a turbine generator.

The waste produced from the manufacturing process is a mixture of cardboard, paper, cotton wool and a small quantity of plastic.

An analysis of the constituents is given in table 4.

In any one load, the proportion of constituents varies greatly and hence so does the bulk density.

The amount of plastic was initially of concern due to the evolution of chlorine and its potential corrosive effects. It was anticipated that the furnace flue gasses would contain in excess of 800 ppm of HCL. Under these conditions the furnace tube surfaces would be most at risk. It was concluded, though, that the low metal temperatures (220 deg C.) would ensure that the problem was not serious. Tube surfaces have been monitored regularly during the operation of the boiler and no evidence of hydrogen chloride corrosion has been found.

Probably, the major problem in the utilisation of the waste is that on a volume basis the material has a relatively low heat content in comparison to other fuels (typically 2,000 MJ/m3, compared with 24,000 MJ/m3 for coal).

Four methods of handling the waste were considered:

o Compressing to form a hard lump
o Shredding to give a light fluffy material
o Shredding and conditioning to form a compact material
o Shredding, conditioning and mixing with bed material to form a compact dense material.

The simple shredding of the material was selected as the proposed handling method. The shredding process is simple and the resultant material is easily transportable by pneumatic methods.

Combustion tests were carried out in a small scale test facility. The material was fed over a fluidised bed. Whilst some of the materials dropped into the bed, the majority burned rapidly in suspension.

Robinson and Son's installed the handling system as shown diagrammatically in figure 4. Waste material is deposited in large plastic bags in each of the various factories. Lorries collect the bags and deliver them to the boiler house. The bags are manhandled from the lorries to the conveyor serving the shredder. The shredder is not sized to accept complete bags of waste, and the operator is required to split them as they are deposited on the conveyor. Manning levels have not been increased for the waste firing facility. All of the waste handling is carried out by the boiler operators in conjunction with their other duties.

After shredding, the material is blown to a large drum which acts as a holding vessel. It is agitated by a rotating blade to prevent any compacting and ensure a homogenous supply. Screw feeders meter the material from the drum into another pneumatic system, which transports it directly into the boiler furnace. Presently only one furnace is being utilised, the waste being admitted through ports in the two

front corners, at a position just above the bed level. (figure 5) It is intended to extend the system to incorporate waste firing in the second furnace, the necessary ports and screw feeders were installed with the original equipment.

Up to 40 tonnes per week of waste is produced within Robinson and Son's. Unless burned in the boiler, this material is dumped with an inherent disposal cost. Presently approximately 10 tonne per week of material is burned and has been for over 4,000 hours. The burning of more is limited by the storage and handling problems due to the bulky nature of the material.

In order to limit excess air levels the final transport air was taken from the F.D. fan. It was found that this limited the fluidising air to the bed, affected bed performance and resulted in high bed temperatures. Subsequently individual fans were installed for the transport lines. Control of the total air is by manual adjustment and care must be taken to retain design excess air levels whilst maintaining acceptable conditions within the bed.

Due to the nature of the fine shredded material, it has been found to "pack" in some area's of the transport system. In this condition it forms a solid mass which is very difficult to remove and continues to accumulate. Minor modifications, particularly an increase in transport air resolved this problem.

Performance tests have been carried out on the plant when burning waste. The results are given in table 5. A reduction of 6.6% in coal usage has been identified when burning waste at 130 kg/h equivalent to 6.7% of total heat input.

The savings made in both waste disposal and coal usage have substantiated the capital expenditure in the plant. An estimated economic analysis of the waste handling system is given in table 6 and shows a payback period of 14.8 months.

Current Status

The system operates satisfactorily and up to 10 tonne per week of waste can be burned on a continuous basis. The actual throughput is limited by the availability of an operator to supply waste to the handling system. It is proposed to increase the automation and hence capacity of the waste firing facility and to integrate it fully into the boiler microprocessor control.

CONCLUSIONS

The first stage of development has been completed. Waste handling and firing systems have been developed for the combustion of two waste fuels with diverse properties. It has been demonstrated that coal usage can be reduced by up to 10% by the combustion of waste fuels.

Savings due to a reduction in primary fuel and disposal costs have been identified, indicating an acceptable payback period for the capital invested. However, a full economic analysis cannot yet be compiled, as the developments are not completed and long term effects cannot yet be assessed.

Before further investment can be made, work is required to consolidate the experience gained and reach a full understanding of the combustion and handling criterion. Periods of monitoring and/or trials may be required to assist in this assessment. Further sponsorship may also be necessary to promote the progress, and release information of use in other applications.

Future developments will address maintenance problems and the integration of the combustion systems into the boiler control, thus allowing unsupervised operation. The main development will be to increase the waste fuel combustion rates and thus cost savings.

ACKNOWLEDGEMENT

This paper is published with the permission of Foster Wheeler Power Products Ltd., Woolcombers Ltd., and Robinson and Sons Ltd., but the views expressed are those of the authors and not necessarily those of the respective companies.

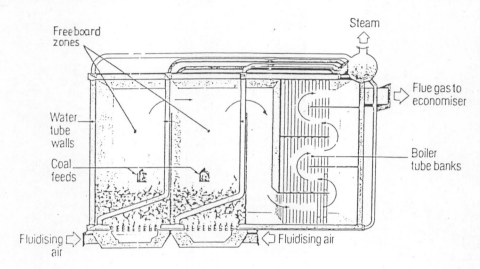

Fig 1   Modular water tube boiler

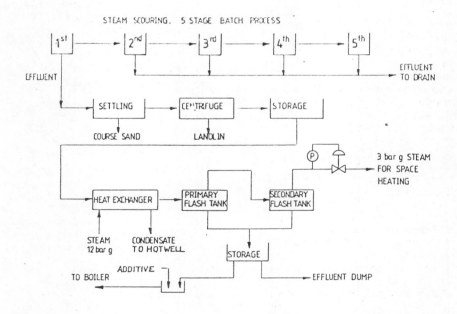

Fig 2   Diagram of woolgrease concentration system at Woolcombers Limited

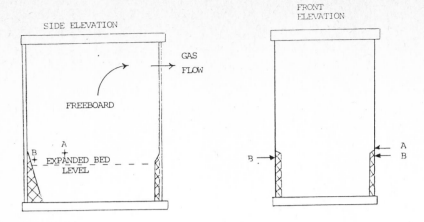

A   INITIAL, SINGLE NOZZLE INJECTION POINT

B   RELOCATION ABOVE EXPANDED BED LEVEL

Fig 3   Location of woolgrease injection points — Woolcombers fluidized bed
         (FB) boiler

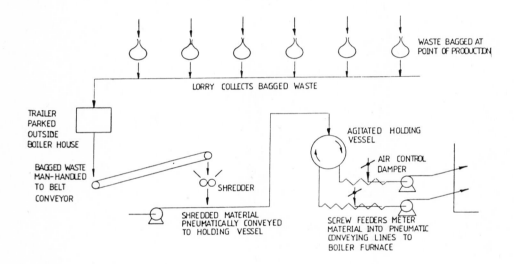

Fig 4   Diagram of waste handling system at Robinsons and Sons Limited

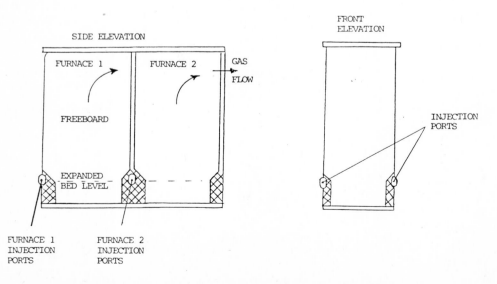

Fig 5   Location of waste firing ports — Robinson and Sons FB boiler

114

© IMechE 1988 C12/88

		WOOLCOMBERS	ROBINSON & SON'S
Boiler Duty	(MW)	7.1	10.2
Boiler Output	(Tonne/h)	11.3	13.6
Steam Outlet Pressure	(barg)	12.4	13.8
Steam Condition		Saturated	Saturated
Gross Efficiency on GCV (coal only)	(%)	83.3	81.5
Feedwater Temperature	(deg C.)	77	65
Economiser exit gas Temperature	(deg C.)	170	170
Design Fluidising Velocity	(m/s)	2.4	2.2
Excess Air	(%)	30	30
Bed Temperature Operating Range	(deg C.)	800-950	800-950
Static Bed Height	(mm)	250	210

Table 1 Nominal boiler operating conditions

DRY ANALYSIS:

ASH	%	31
ORGANIC MATTER	%	69

ELEMENTAL ANALYSIS:

mg/l

SILICON	3,300
ALUMINIUM	2,450
IRON	1,490
SODIUM	3,700
CALCIUM	1,600
MAGNESIUM	680
PHOSPHOROUS	20
POTASSIUM	52,050

GROSS CALORIFIC VALUE   20,930 kj/kg DRY

TYPICAL WATER CONTENT   64% (as fired)

Table 2 Analysis of woolgrease effluent

PERIOD	STEAM RAISED T	COAL BURNED T	WOOLGREASE BURNED l	STEAM COAL RATIO	TYPICAL F.E.T. DEG.C.	TYPICAL STACK TEMP DEG C.
A	1,318	135	–	9.76	720	168
B	782.8	73.4	21,140	10.66	750	179

PRIMARY FUEL SAVING FROM WOOLGREASE = 9.3%

Table 3 Typical operating data — Woolcombers FB boiler

Constituent Analysis   wt % (dry)

        Cardboard   9
        Plastic   20
        Cotton Wool   71
        Moisture Content   4   (as received)

Calorific Values
                                            kj/kg (dry)

        Cardboard   15,550
        Plastic   34,200
        Rag Waste   15,700

Size Distribution

        Cardboard   up to 50mm Square
        Plastic   up to 30mm Square
        Cotton Wool   up to 100mm Cube

Table 4 Analysis of waste material — Robinson and Sons

PERIOD	HEAT INPUT	GROSS EFFICIENCY	COAL BURNED	WASTE BURNED	TYPICAL F.E.T. DEG.C.	TYPICAL STACK TEMP. DEG.C.
	MW	%	T	T		
A	10.57	80.8	6.38	–	660	170
B	10.60	80.5	5.96	0.67	680	170

PRIMARY FUEL SAVING FROM WASTE = 6.6%

Table 5 Typical operating data — Robinson and Sons FB boiler

CAPITAL AND INSTALLATION
COST   £31,000

SAVINGS:

        WASTE DISPOSAL   £13,000
        PRIMARY FUEL   £22,700

COSTS:

        POWER   £10,600
                                                  ─────────
                        NET ANNUAL SAVING   £25,100

                        PAYBACK 14.8 MONTHS

BASIS:

        1) 4000 Waste burning hours per annum
        2) 6% reduction on primary fuel
        3) System maintenance not included
        4) System manned by existing boiler operators

Table 6 Estimated payback analysis waste handling system — Robinson and
         Sons FB boiler